Ain't No Mountain High Enough

From Disability to Possibility

Hanneke Boot

AuthorHouse™ UK
1663 Liberty Drive
Bloomington, IN 47403 USA
www.authorhouse.co.uk
Phone: 0800 047 8203 (Domestic TFN)
+44 1908 723714 (International)

Because of the dynamic nature of the Internet, any web addresses or links contained in this book may have changed since publication and may no longer be valid. The views expressed in this work are solely those of the author and do not necessarily reflect the views of the publisher, and the publisher hereby disclaims any responsibility for them.

Any people depicted in stock imagery provided by Getty Images are models, and such images are being used for illustrative purposes only.
Certain stock imagery © Getty Images.

This book is printed on acid-free paper.

ISBN: 978-1-7283-9824-2 (sc)
ISBN: 978-1-7283-9823-5 (e)

Print information available on the last page.

Published by AuthorHouse 05/08/2020

authorHOUSE®

Preface

When I'm eighteen, I discover that painting with my mouth is easier for me than painting with my hands. Through a colleague friend, I come in contact with the International Association of Mouth and Foot Painters. For me a source of inspiration.

I currently have three assignments for painting a portrait. On my easel is an acrylic painting of a young girl with blond long hair. My expression is true to the photo behind it. On the walls in my house hang my watercolours and acrylic paintings of flowers and animals and an icon next to the work of a painter who was once my teacher.

I paint everything: views, landscapes, mills and portraits. As long as it is not abstract work. With a brush in my mouth, I deftly pick up some paint that I smear on my canvas with rapid head movements.

Courses

Around the age of eighteen, suffering from a muscle disease, I discovered that painting with my mouth was easier for me than painting with my hands. Only perspective painting was difficult. To learn more, I started a painting course in my neighbourhood. Soon painting caught me in such a way that I also started taking other painting courses and I focused more and more on painting. I hung up My psychology studies at the open university at the time.

During an exhibition I came across another mouth painter: Kees Schut. He wanted to register with the International Association of Mouth and Foot Painters and asked whether I was interested. I found Kees' work so beautiful and qualitatively so much better than mine that I didn't dare to do well.

Artist organization

The roots of the International Association of Mouth and Foot Painters are in the dwarf state of Liechtenstein. There the mouth painter Arnulf Erich Stegman, together with seventeen other artists, founded an artists' organization in 1956. They experienced first-hand what it means to be dependent on care and help from others. It deeply affected their autonomy and personal freedom.

The artists' organization grew into an international association of which 780 mouth and foot painters from 74 countries are currently members. From the outset, the motto of this association was: "No pity." Now she supports fifty artists who work with their mouths and / or feet because of their disability or illness.

Seven times a year the association organizes a worldwide exhibition where it sells work by its artists. She publishes art cards, diaries, calendars and reproductions via publishing houses. She awards scholarships to prospective members and grants to members so that they can buy good materials. The condition is that they continue to develop and develop. Because the association places high artistic demands on its members. They must be able to compete with other artists on the international art market.

Stock market

About twenty years ago, I was called by the International Association of Mouth and Foot Painters in Liechtenstein. Whether I wanted to become a member of this association. Kees Schut, also a mouth painter, had passed on my name. Afterwards it turned out that they only had two members in the Netherlands at the time. So, they were happy that I worked that way.

I had to send my work to Liechtenstein. I was admitted to the association and received a scholarship. For that I have to buy materials and take painting lessons. It helps me to work with good paints and to present my work in beautiful frames and passe-partouts.

In return, I regularly provide work and have to make the association more known through publicity and giving lectures. Sometimes the association sells its paintings on the other side of the world. I even received a stack of cards that were issued in Canada with my drawing on it, and now paintings of winter landscapes are going out again for prints on Christmas cards.

Inspiration

A number of times, I was invited by the association to an international meeting. Sometimes four hundred mouth and foot painters approached them with whom I spoke, debated, attended workshops and worked for five to seven days.

These meetings inspire me enormously. I meet people there who work under much more primitive conditions than I do. Some of them should beg to stay alive without the support of the International Association of Mouth and Foot Painters. If I have a hard time and I don't like painting, I think of them and I know I just have to keep going.

Meanwhile, I'm becoming increasingly famous. Once a week I'm on the road for a lecture at various associations, organizations and schools. And sometimes I'm invited to television programs such as tattoo artist, painter and writer Henk Schiffmacher who later auctioned my work in nightclub Panama in Amsterdam.

For my lectures, I collected slides about how I painted and played music with my sister as a child. I use the film that a filmmaker made about my life and give demonstrations with my assistance dog.

I can also get a salary from the International Association of Mouth and Foot Painters, but for that I have to deliver a constant production. I find that difficult. Because I love company too much to fully concentrate on that.

Chapter 1

In tension at home 25-01-2015 3:40 pm.

It is unbelievable, but it is so encouraging, because even people I barely know, wish me much strength or send me a card from the place where I gave a lecture. One more day and then I will hear if the operation will go ahead ... but I really want it to go on anyway. It is sometimes hard to harden. Pain makes you so terribly tired and depressed, but I still want so much, so much. I also almost miss out on time now, writing. It will be night work. Payments just out the door, important letters but sending mail, is faster. Soon I will try to see if I can clamber in the Corsa of a very good friend [Intimate 'magic man'] who will take me to the hospital. My paintings still have to leave the house for the mouth and foot painters. I want to pack my suitcase today, tomorrow I will also have everything ... you will see. Now a quick cup of tea ...

How nice all those phone calls, cards and emails at the last minute. Now it must go on though. I'm so nervous about tomorrow. I will transfer my phone to my cell phone, as I will be on the road all day tomorrow and will certainly not want to miss the announcement from the hospital.

The fitting in the Corsa has actually succeeded. Seat in the rear position, backrest almost lying down ... is this the Bold feeling? Or a sardine that is canned? Well, I really had that feeling with such an old little Fiat model. And now I had the teeth together with boarding, but when I look at the driver again everything is ok. Nice walk just in the freezing cold with Luigi my service dog. I Got tears in my eyes, cold ... emotional, full ... or it is full moon? It seemed beautiful and even the shadow side was lit. Must be a good sign ...

And just trying to transfer my nice welcome text on my cell phone, I got an English-speaking guy every time. No wonder nobody had left a voice. Thought it was a wrong number. So, early this morning to the phone store to ask what is wrong, because nothing wanted to transfer anymore. Imagine that the VUMC hospital is just calling. Indeed, there appeared to be a wrong communication with Vodafone. Fifteen minutes of puzzling there and it was done. And yes ... I just put my car on the path with my parents and I am just on my way with my wheelchair to the community centre to make my weekly press releases, I am standing at the traffic lights with a lot of noise ... a call. With my thick mittens on my hands too late to record, but luckily, my nice welcome text saves me. It was the VUMC if I want to come tomorrow in the afternoon. Even though it is still so exciting, a burden fell off my shoulders. In a few days I will be in possession of a second new hip. In the evening I had dinner with my parents [gallows meal] also in the community centre, simple but very nutritious. Three courses, typically Dutch and tasty. Cappuccino after.

For also done my last choral rehearsal. Nice distraction. Still talking to a member who had been driving with me for the first time with the car. She thought it was wonderful, a rotating wheel without touching it with one finger. Hey, joystick, pneumatic door opener and tailgate opener, central locking, no double airbag, great car ... cup of coffee? I don't feel like sleeping at all, if I can sleep at all. Have some nice music on, go cuddle with my animals and if I go to bed late enough there will probably be time to pack something, because then the rest will be flat. My list is already ready.

Oh solo mio ... if only I had someone around me. Hang on a little longer. Tomorrow morning nice coffee table with parents and friends dear to me. A strange feeling. Say a little goodbye.

Just another life later. Does not have to be boring! New goals, new challenges, new victories. Live life too and don't let it pass you by. Not superficial but depth. It storms me and it shapes me. The courage and the struggle make me who I always am and want to stay. I always want to continue even though it takes tears. My nature is too curious what life could bring me. A bit of excitement is also a bit of adventure ...

It's been night long. Will have to be well rested tomorrow [later] ... go to my bed.

Refresh memory VUMC Hospital 01-02-2015 16: 03h.
Thursday would be a pleasant coffee morning, but according to the bystanders I was not that pleasant. Continuous telephone. One was not ready yet or the other reported [ISDN]. I had different ideas about saying goodbye to my dog. Hold on to the bed. All at the last minute on the toilet. A lick over my face. My 'lovely' driver had already driven and the seat was already in 'the elite feeling'. Fortunately, I had not had a moment to worry. I didn't want to do that either now, so I just looked at the driver and we talked about PCs, etc. As if it had to be that way, there was one disabled parking place free

near the hospital. The department apparently also waited, while we were right on time. Swallowing was that I was not operated on by 'my' professor, but by a Belgian Moroccan and a Nigerian [who looked a bit like Eddy Murphy] who seemed very calming. It is of course not the first time for me hanging around in hospitals, so the question arose whether I had a medical education. Then the mood was in.

Blood sampling was a downfall. About five people did not succeed. I was so glad that this nice friend was still there. Courage fell. Just before dinner the anaesthetist himself came to take five tubes of blood through the groin. Ouch ... not tasty. When I returned to the hall, my food had also disappeared. Looking, because now I was hungry. A bit of cosy food ... then it's time to say goodbye. Hey why do I always get a lump in my throat when he has to leave ...please stay.

In the evening, I have to take a shower and then go to bed. Slept? Maybe the last hour.

Refresher Friday VUMC Hospital 02-02-2015 15: 55h.
'Mrs. Boot?' [10x]. Had I certainly fallen asleep? Showering again, mandatory. Yummy. OK apron and there I were ready and waiting. "You can go to the recovery room." Is that the right order? After such a bad night ... All kinds of patients were moaning and recovering. I prefer to look at the Winnie de Poe poster, hanging on a red balloon. Delicious. I didn't have much time to fantasize, because my bed was set in motion along Ok 1, Ok 2, 3, 4 ... so much? It became room 5. A cold room as I thought. With my breath I still tested if I saw condensation, but it wasn't that cold either. I had to sit on a narrow bench. Did everything have to happen there? It was explained how the gas cap worked, so that I no longer feared the necessary search for a vein. Three times fresh air in and out, with the last breath ... "yes now the cap please." And three conscious breaths. Away! After three more conscious breaths, I regained knowledge, but four hours in between. "Do you have pain?" Fairly. Inject one into the drip. "Are you sick?" Inject two into the drip. This just went on three times. After I was free of complaints, I could even go back to Orthopaedics. Mom and dad arrived a little while, although I wasn't very talked about. Nice anyway.

A little pace at VUMC Hospital 03-02-2015 16: 27h.
You don't even turn a blind eye that night after the operation. Occasionally it seemed as if I was in the tropics. First in terms of temperature, I really let the sister occasionally flutter with the sheet to let me cool down.

Then trembling and rattling sounds of vipers and the sawmill that just continues. And then you finally sleep, wake up again to have the blood pressure measured. When I also see an older lady in the morning with big sunglasses, who apparently turned out to be strong, you just don't know anymore. The only thing I can do then is laugh terribly mealy. That also discharges. When people are asked what to laugh about, I say that the TV is so nice.

Sunday I wanted to see a different wallpaper and do something about my mental health. It's just about me being in the same boat and having to deal with it in your own way. But the atmosphere and the way of dealing with each other gives a different feeling. And in my way I hope to be a light for someone else.

In the afternoon, dad and mom are faithfully visiting again.

Even before the crowds started in the evening, the physiotherapist stood next to my bed, while my second cousin [the webmaster], who did not even recognize me, arrived with his girlfriend. The physiotherapist wanted me out of bed. Ho, ho. X-ray first! Well, then on the edge of the bed. The visitors moved away for a moment; the 'tent' was closed. I was pulled off the side of my operated leg. Oh, it hurt so much. I sat, but don't ask how. Sweat broke out ... At that moment 'my guardian angel' magic man suddenly popped through the curtains. What a timing! I don't know how it happened, but I just got enough puff to say, "I'm already sitting." After the greeting, my bed seemed nicer than ever. But I had been sitting. And so, we always go a little further.

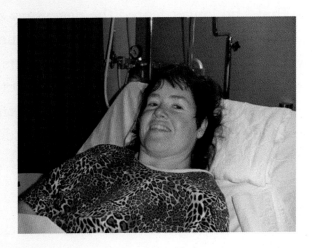

Something from the VUMC Amsterdam webmaster 03-02-2015 21: 45h.
At exactly 4 o'clock we arrived in the room where Hanneke had to be. She had dyed her hair so I didn't even recognize her. Hanneke was very pleased; the operation went very

well. A new method has been applied so that no muscles have to be run through. This will probably make the recovery much smoother. After five minutes the physiotherapist came and Hanneke actually had to get out of bed and we of course went into the corridor. She did not dare to get out of bed because the X-rays taken after the operation failed. She wants to know for sure that it is possible before she stands up. Now sitting on the edge of bed was enough. For her it was already much more than she thought possible. She would like to write in her diary herself, but that was not yet possible. Once it is settled you can expect something from her again.

Standing and going VUMC hospital 04-02-2015 3:32 pm.

Fortunately, the days go a bit faster, but the night's stay long. I also want to continue to see my alarm clock to see how long time remains until the morning. Once there was a cup of water in front of it and for that I called the night shift and first asked for a sip of water of course.

Today another exciting day. I had to get out and I had to stand. The X ray was fine. Both shoes on, crutches under my arms, carefully upright. Clearly something is wrong. The operated leg was completely crooked and inward. It hurt a lot and it was clearly much longer. It just wasn't my leg. I tried to move myself a little, but it really didn't work that way. Exhausted again in bed, my mind wandered how this should continue. Tonight, I have plenty of time to think about it ...

Big leaps 'backwards' VUMC hospital 04-02-2015 16: 15h.

The following idea seemed the best for me to try. On a shoe and an old soccer shoe. On the right the shoe and on the left my soccer shoe. So, the length difference was pretty well resolved. I could stand with two legs straight. Really burdening the leg still hurts. That brings with it, hopefully, a temporary difficulty. When my left hip was replaced 9 years ago, the front muscles had to be cut otherwise it would keep shooting out of the bowl. The result is that the force has not been used to move the leg forwards, unless of course I am fully loaded on the right. The muscles do it backwards so we just started going backwards. My weird sense of humour ran away with me again. I will soon say to the visitors: 'it is deteriorating fast'. And many people came to visit. 'Him' too. But because of all the impressions, I just wanted to get away from the room here. Enjoying the four of them at the restaurant at my expense. I think it was well used and what a cup of cappuccino. It seemed like soup bowls. My own cup was half of it so I thought I deserved a second one.

So I had a bit of distraction again. I do not yet feel myself and my leg either. The pain increased dramatically. May I have one more thing please? Just be alone with 'him'? I wanted to go back to bed. Wash up. A beautiful laptop on my lap in bed. Interesting to study. I actually wanted to put my arms around him spontaneously, but they can't, won't and don't. No courage to ask. I do love him so. My suggestion was to open the room door as wide as possible to keep eye contact as long as it could when he left. I put the sheet between my teeth and bit it, pulled it up so that my head could get under it. Just leave me alone. I wanted to think of beautiful things ... as long as everything is fine again.

Anxiety VUMC Hospital 07-02-2015 15: 39h.

A new patient came to my side last night. I think she was a lot younger than me. In fact, we all didn't realize how nervous she was. She was always gone. Early in the morning I suddenly caught the conversation between her and the orthopaedist. At first, she was in doubt and almost wanted to go home, but in my opinion, she was not sufficiently informed. The orthopaedist now had a five-hour operation, so I assumed she had five hours of reflection. She was so alone. I had to take action by myself and asked through the screen curtain if I could do something for her and if she could ask me anything she could. That's how she stood by my bed for a while to talk to me. The other patients also took care of this girl and so we tried to encourage her. She was damned to hear a few hours later that the orthopaedist abandoned the operation because a patient had to stand 100% behind the operation and he preferred a conversation. Then she was even more upset and it also affected the mood in our room. But I can imagine how she felt after our chat. With fear you are all alone. Nobody can feel that and cannot take it away from you. No matter how many operations this is, I also keep terrible fear. You have to be able to totally surrender to people, equipment, technology, gases, etc. My mother and I even talked about dying a day before the operation while walking with Luigi. That I wanted to be in a white funeral car, then wanted to be buried near Nero my first dog, then Luigi next to me later. Weird isn't it?

I called a friend who had also seen me here two years ago in the VUMC. Outrageous, but he still came to see me again in his motor suit. He couldn't resist sitting in the sports wheelchair of my girlfriend who was just feeding me fruit and he was balancing through the hall on 2 wheels. Very laughable. Together with my girlfriend we immediately made an appointment for a performance by his dance group, because the next time does not have to be in the hospital again according to him. It is mid-April in a weekend. Would I be on my feet then? Bet...?

All corners of the room VUMC Hospital 07-02-2015 16: 16h.

The bed beside me was gone! Right in front of me too and diagonally opposite me was a pleasant woman with whom I had chatted last night until after 01:00 h. The night does not last that long. This day was very strange. In the afternoon I was suddenly driven away with my bed to another room. There was a foreign woman whose husband was just pacing from hall to hall. For a while I was waiting for my other roommate to come. She also came but told sadly that she decided to go home. Otherwise she would go after the weekend. As a consolation, I gave her, my own postcard and my mobile number. Who knows, I can soon leave too. I didn't have TV at the moment. Could I spend 45 minutes across the street in front of TV then I was put back in my corner. A constantly complaining woman next to me. How could I ever sleep? I kept my headphones on all night for the radio to pass by.

I wanted to leave in the morning. Headache. I was the first to be helped this Sunday. "Take me to the chapel!" With the first song the tears rolled down my cheeks. God, I want so much. Are you still there?"

We went shopping with mom and dad. Can be here too in hospital. A few shops. I Bought a nice doll like Annie M G Smidt for in the window frame.

When I was in bed again and I was annoyed by the ice-black man dressed up, I thought; if he does look like a James, he can also extend his hands for me. "Sir, can you do something for me please?" "Yes, sure madame. what can I do for you?" Oh, that sounds good, let me serve you. "I'm a little bit cold, can you do my blanket higher?" Between the thumbs and forefingers, he grabbed the sheet and lifted it up. "Anything else madame?" Now I had to watch out, because if I thought about something, I would burst out laughing (a kiss on my cheek?), I might have such a change in mood swings. "Not at the moment, thank you very much." My headache was over.

E.R. VUMC Hospital 09-02-2015 16: 01h.

It is really a company here. In the middle of the night, ambulance staff brought a lady. Strangely enough, in my opinion with regard to privacy, all questions were asked and tests were done in the hall. But the questions turned out to be important if she would be operated on tonight. That also happened. Pretty impressive.

The next morning I was also taken away for an echo of my left arm. It had become much fatter. Two years ago, that indicated thrombosis. After the treatment, I said that my pyjamas could stay off since I still had to be washed. A brother and a sister picked me up again. The brother's gaze fell on the pyjamas at the foot of the bed. "How are you actually doing?" I laughed immediately. "Yes?" "Yes, like that." I confirmed and laughed again. Men! Ha-ha.

The day also had a serious character. I started talking to a man who first had to have all kinds of investigations. He was already in a wheelchair and had a great deal of functional loss due to a tumour. He faced very difficult minutes today. Either the operation continues with reasonably good chances for a viable life or the operation did not continue and to live for a few more years. Somehow it clicked and I noticed that our character traits did not differ much from each other. We talked for a while and when he got the message that the operation went ahead, I was so happy for him that I gave my book.

'Dear people, tomorrow I will go to Rehabilitation Centre. Hopefully there is internet connection. Otherwise I try to arrange something.

But one thing, make something beautiful every day.'

The move Wijk aan Zee 12-02-2015 8:51 p.m.
Rehabilitation centre

I Slightly woke up with a headache after an emergency night.

I didn't eat so much on purpose and drank half a cup of chocolate milk and waited an hour for the ambulance that would take me to the Rehabilitation Centre, straight and as if in a straitjacket I lay on a stretcher. The further we got, the more nauseous I became and I asked if there were any spit trays. "You lie on it, just sigh deeply". I felt that this would not go well and just before Wijk aan Zee I reported that I did not like it anymore. "Stop!" cried the brother to his colleague, because I felt sick. Half a glass of chocolate milk seemed to have been multiplied by a litter bottle in my stomach. The right-side door was pushed open by the ambulance brother and luckily, I got some fresh air. I was so embarrassed. Do I have that luck? The rest of the journey went on to the Rehabilitation Centre. When I was unloaded there, I really got the fresh air from Wijk aan Zee, the wind howling around my ears. While checking in, which the ambulance brother did, an electric wheelchair tore at me. It was the ex-revalidated neighbour who had a room next to me 2 years ago. I had the strong impression that he was happy to see me again. I got a pat on my cheek, that was a great consolation to all the commotion. I spent the rest of the day in bed.

Recognition Wijk aan Zee 12-02-2015 20: 58h.

After a wonderful shower, I was brought to the walking (rolling) buffet in a Rehabilitation centre wheelchair. This already feels a lot better than in the hospital. Due to lack of time I had the intake interview with the physiotherapist during my breakfast. After lunch one of my friends brought my electric wheelchair. Naturally, I was put into it. Great, that way I was nice and mobile again and went on rides through the entire building. And what I had expected a little, I heard here and there, "hey Hanneke, what brings you here?" Whatever I have explained. What I was especially looking forward to was that Luigi my service dog would come in the evening with my girlfriend. I was very curious how he would react. The bus arrived there and Luigi was the first to arrive. I whistled with the familiar flute tune in front of him, his ears were immediately pinned, his head was all searching. He ran to the first sliding doors that opened, but the second door does not open until the first closes. He was so excited. Fortunately, he had not forgotten me. I gave him the command to make him jump on my lap, but it seemed as if he felt that it is actually not possible. He remained very careful and stood stiffly beside the wheelchair. I was able to tickle his fur nicely with my hand. So, I can enjoy my dog for two hours. The people in my department have already been able to get to know him, to prepare them in two weeks then he will stay with me. That will be fine.

I Start to feel at home again Wijk aan Zee 12-02-2015 9: 1 pm.

I Started with a nice breakfast with a croissant and a fried egg. A good start to the day. Then another exciting moment, out of the 27 stitches, they took 17 out of it, alternately. Because here and there, there is still some tension on the wound. I wanted to see what it looked like once in a while and shuffled with my crutches to the mirror under the supervision of nursing, because I'm not that stable yet. The length of the scar was not that bad. Afternoon visit by my 'magic man'. It was a race against the clock again, time passed so quickly. I Just given him homework on his laptop for my diary. Has he already written something down, since I can't use the keyboard on the ward here yet? There is an internet connection but I still have to think about how I can operate it myself. Unfortunately, I was already called to come to the supper. Now I had energy again for ten of this pleasant visits. Dinner was also on the fancy side. The nursing staff went around with a large bowl of herring with onions. In the meantime, I also get better contact with the rehabilitation staff in my department. That evening I had some phone calls on my cell phone and so I am back all day without resting, so …. progress made !!!

Spa? Wijk aan Zee 14-02-2015 6:51 pm.

What a stormy weather last night. We are really on the coast here. The room creaked completely. Despite that, I only sleep well here. My roommate was away all weekend.

It is not the first time that I have been here, but I am still being pampered to get used to something. First delicious breakfast. After that I was sitting in my room listening to a coffee concert. And what does that include? Coffee. Spontaneously the coffee with my adjustment and all neatly delivered: room service. I was also asked to try out a special toilet, because the normal toilet there I hung more than I sat. It is a toilet that can be raised and lowered as a whole. Rinses, continues and it blows when you're done. Almost like being at home, so I feel more and more at home.

What also gave me a recreational feeling was that the Dutch broadcast had a break for a walking program in the canteen of the Rehabilitation Centre. Nice and busy with all walkers. Of course, I was recognized again. When not? A man, my age stood in the elevator with me and told me that we had played with each other about 35 years ago. The association here, of course, I could not explain who it was. Probably at home. When he said so I saw it. He lived one street further. His and my parents still live that street further. Weird world.

In the afternoon a visit of another friend with an assistance dog. Yes, once you are in possession of such a dog, you also get more acquaintances with such a dog. They just have to get used to that. They are very sweet animals.

Furthermore, this day went well.

Winter coat Wijk aan Zee 14-02-2015 19: 26h.

The place to meet is in the canteen and I saw several watching. "Is it her or isn't she her?" I just said it was my winter fur and that I am blond again in the summer. The floor was also searched. There was even talk of a holy duality so inseparable with my dog, but another 1.5 weeks. Then he stays.

Today I think I walked 6 meters at physiotherapy. With all the steps I do, I still feel more secure and the pain gradually disappears. I experience it as a great adventure how it will continue. Life is also an adventure; I love adventure and I also look for it when I get the feeling that I need more excitement in my life. If I want to go for something, don't postpone it later or for too long. Then it may be too late. When I had driving lessons, I had to get my driver's license. If I like someone, I want to say it now, full of conviction. When a playback show is being held here, like 2 years ago, I want to win it. I came across the organizer. He said there was no playback show last year due to spending cuts. So ... after me there has been no winner. So, I can't get away from it. At least I have to defend my title. Whether I am already gone or not (April 20: playback show) I get permission to participate. Fun! Just go crazy. The choice has been made. Participate.

Hanneke in action Texel 15-02-2015 7:40 pm.
To prove that Hanneke is recovering, here are a few photos.

First she slowly gets out of bed ......
..... and then she walks a bit.
Hanneke, a lot of strength on behalf of your 'MAGIC MAN' and the webmaster

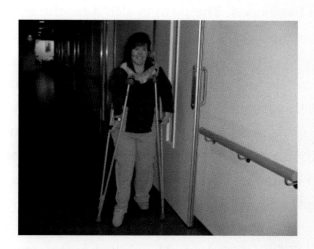

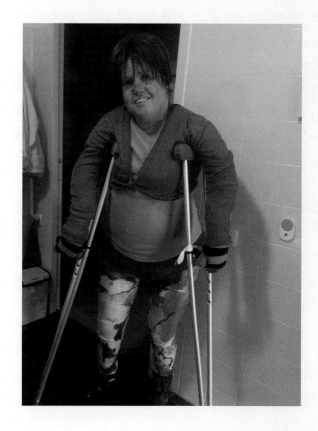

Fitting and measuring Wijk aan Zee 16-02-2015 9:17 pm.

The day started well. My wheelchair was at the charger last night with the cord neatly in the wheelchair, but not in the socket. More than half empty. I Put the wheelchair on the charger during lunch. Afterwards, when I was waiting for occupational therapy, nobody showed up there. It turned out to be sick. Fine, was I racing like that before? At physiotherapy I wanted to know how much leg length difference I had. So, it appears to be 2.5 cm. Quite a lot. That means that a lot of things have to change with that. The left shoe equally high, the footrests 2.5 cm lower. The stools extend a hole. Yes, with me everything is millimetre work. Every change can turn out wrong or disadvantageous for me and therefore it has to be adjusted again. I immediately went after it. It already feels a lot firmer with two shoes. The pain is still a bit the same. By the way, 9 stitches have not been removed.

Luigi came again. Now he knew immediately that I was waiting for him and he was very intrusive now at the second sliding doors and started barking with impatience. It is now more difficult for him to say goodbye. He jumped neatly in the front of the bus and jumped out again to run to the door. Up to 3 times, so that fellow invalidates even got a lump in their throat. But I could not get over my heart to leave either. I wanted to say goodbye to them all.

I now type again myself for a few days. The right-hand part of the keyboard is slanted on the armrest of the wheelchair. The left-hand part is on a chessboard which lies on the lap diagonally through the table [can you now play chess?], So the mouse cannot slide away due to the raised edge. It takes me some effort, sweat is on my back, but my entire condition must also go ahead. This way I cannot come forward to sit up straight. I don't get my legs on the footrests myself. With food I am first being pushed forward and my arm is placed around my dining table, so that I don't fall back too quickly. Keep practicing!!!

Striking Wijk aan Zee 19-02-2015 11: 25h.

So many reactions are always: "what, you look good". I am sure that this means not only that I am nice and sturdy, but I will also come across as much more relaxed. After all, the pain is getting less and less. I'm Sitting and lying almost not at all. Only with walking still. It is also scary to tax. But now it is almost a day and night difference. The last half year it became worse by the week you can say. The worse it got, the busier I made my program to be able to forget and be busy with. Sometimes until late at night I was still sketching, writing or sitting at the PC. I did say that I was in pain, but didn't really show the appearance. But because I knew that I would be operated on anyway, I thought maybe too lightly about it. "I care if I work or break, I can rest in the hospital later." To be honest, I was also pretty demolished just before the operation. A lot of pain and I became depressed. Everywhere I started to look up. Then I found it quite difficult to be assertive enough to show others my insecurity and sorrow. Some of them have got to know a completely different side of me, but so have I. How sweet and worried they were to me. Pain is simply very difficult for someone else to estimate. I think another person might feel very powerless then. That powerlessness then feels shared at that moment. I am so happy that the pain is gradually decreasing. I will soon be a different person. My bookings just go through here. Work back on the shop, but no pain.

The last stitches are now out. There is still a small open wound that is neatly cared for. I Walked 12 meters yesterday. With my armpit crutches that protrude 2 meters high, I drive to the physiotherapy. What stand out!

New strength Wijk aan Zee 21-02-2015 14: 08h.
Quite easy if you are already fairly familiar here. To be honest, the intervening periods are getting shorter and shorter. Hopefully this will not continue in this line. The 1st time here was 1981, the 2nd time 1995, the 3rd time in 2002 and then 2005, 2007 and now 2015. Anyway, now that my program still looks very calm, I have probably received a list of the sports when something is on which day and time that I can participate. A so-called 'wild card'? And then of course try to win.

Oh, I am so happy that the pain is getting less and less. A small piece of the scar is not completely healed and standing still hurts my right buttock. This morning my physiotherapist checked the status of what happened during the operation. Muscles seem to have been diverted and attached to something else. That must of course cure.

I have often thought about my pain and how to express it. My concerns about the pain, but also thoughts and uncertainty about whether expressing it would take away the attractiveness and charms of me. I always want to be cheerful and strong for everyone, that's happy in me. But now I think about a certain person who has come my way, so that I also got extra energy, but also wanted to invest extra energy. Because my pains were a little distracted. A chat, a phone call, a visit, etc. But it was very difficult for me to see another side of me, now that I was so strong. I sometimes told him, expressed. How nice it was to be together to forget the pain and just love each other. But how do you explain that you are about to collapse in pain and prefer to howl, without being a heap of misery, an 'invalid', because I don't feel that way at all inside. A person with a lot of pain at that moment. But it looks like I also have a lot to learn, because why should I be abandoned? After all, I didn't ask for it either. You simply need someone, to have someone around you who puts an arm around your shoulder. I don't have to be ashamed of that. And fortunately, I don't experience it as something unattractive. I was just scared of it. Until the very last moment I also waited to express this, but again I did not find this entirely honest of myself. I was not operated on for nothing, so I had reasons enough to show another side. Now I have learned from it again. But I still want to show character, because that side is simply stronger and more trusted. In this situation of friendship that teaches me a lot, I also want to keep putting energy in. That I will not let myself be put under the table, that I will not just give up and that I see every progress as victory again. Nothing comes with ease. Keep training. Do not put my wheelchair next to my bed when it is time for bed, but put it in the hallway to walk to my bed, with crutches. I've Been outside to 'harden' for when Luigi comes. My 'magic man' came up with the great idea to balance with the walking stick

Luigi Wijk aan Zee 24-02-2015 11: 02h.

First a big move to a private room. The other room that I shared with an older man was really a men's room. He seemed to be quite rich with his perfume or aftershave. I smelled it all day long. Everything was deposited on my bed. Completely full. What I had collected for two weeks, I say to stuff. It even had to add an extra trolley. And I actually had a lot to do in the morning so I couldn't even be there to help with arranging. I think every day is still very quiet. I had already indicated that I felt more like a recreational person than a rehabilitation person. Get up quietly in the morning, poodle [with a nurse sometimes], ongoing buffet. Then a trip through the building to the 'bar' to have a cup of coffee. Sometimes in the morning physiotherapy, I walk half an hour with a break. When there is no physiotherapy there is a ball of jeu des boules. Nice for a while, because I was busy last year. But I am more of the calibre who likes to tackle. Don't complain too long or think about anything, but put your shoulders back. To work. There is still too much to experience in my life.

A day can take a long time if you are waiting for your four-legged friend. Of course, I am aware of it all day long, he only sees it when he sees me. But that feeling you get when you see that he can almost jump through the windows. With such a beast [also with my previous dog, a little more I believe] you have something so close and real. Animals can see your real inside or can feel that. So far, I have had that with all kinds of animals. When I used to ride a horse, I only had to whisper [horse whisperer ha-ha] and it did what I wanted. When I got my first cat, I shouted: "on your pole" and he raced to the cat pole so I could feed him. Now that I have three, it is: "Mandy, Mercy, Felix!

on your pole!" They all fly to their own pole. Summertime when they are outside and I don't want to be embarrassed too much, or I leave myself in that delusion, I shout outside: "Mandy, Mercy, Felix … Supper!"

In the afternoon still a visit from my parents and my girlfriend and the dogs and her driver who also drives me home this weekend. Nice cup of tea I drunk with a chocolate. I'll Show my dog everywhere. Everyone would like to pet him of course. But unfortunately, there is one crossbar that is more often in the drama department and prefers to keep its own rules everywhere, which I understand. But with a stroke the behaviour can get worse and more intense. There seems to have been a Hell's Angels friends club here. In consultation with the nursing staff, I have said, as long as they're still here [until Wednesday, 5 days yet] that I would rather eat in my own room. I just cannot stand that. Hopefully fellow invalidates will come to mind a little when they hear that through them, it isolates me to get no problems and that I just don't want to leave my dog alone. That much means that animal to me. He is my extension, my right hand. Everyone asked here in the house for a reason from the first day that I am here where the dog was now and when it was allowed to come. Now that he is there I will stay with him and he with me. In the evening I actually hung at the bar. Someone from the department said goodbye and I was able to air my heart and have a nice red wine. Toasting on her goodbye and the arrival of Luigi.

First weekend at home Wijk aan Zee 28-02-2015 14: 04h.

After another wonderful walk in the sun and the dunes nice and early I left for my own place. But first we drove past the pastry shop, because this first weekend at home in such a short time was best celebrated with a pastry. Three pieces. The driver did not turn the pastry off and today I was in the company of a travel friend Pierre, who cannot be compared to anyone else and who is ready for me a lot. I really thought it was great that he wanted to assist me on my first weekend as a technical man, but also as a friend. I think those are beautiful moments that make my life that little bit different. After having coffee, I first create some space in my office to be able to use my wheelchair behind the PC, temporarily of course. In the kitchen, my 'ironing stool' was put a hole higher. Later in the day on another second-hand wheelchair, the footrests were made longer, because if the weather is nice the following weekend, I can tour with my girlfriend. Together we did the groceries in the afternoon with the dogs, Pierre also has a Retriever. Then the 'cook' would show his cooking skills and I have already suggested if I can stand well again that I also want to show my cooking skills one time. On my own I don't care about the food in the way it is served. I am satisfied with a quick pack. If only I have food. But to make it for someone is much more fun.

If I do it then I want to do it right. Three courses and a cosy atmosphere. We will see that again. Now I cannot even get out of my wheelchair alone and can only move with two crutches. Then I have my hands full. A nice goal to practice.

In the afternoon we watched a DVD until dinner with a nice glass of wine. Just a festive touch on the first weekend at home. After dinner it was time to say goodbye again and enjoyed a little dreamy. In fact, it seemed that I had not left this place. It's all going differently. I am more dependent, but the idea that it is temporary gives me some reassurance.

I slept wonderfully in my own bed with hugging cats, who clearly had missed me. The youngest also sat on my lap a lot. This day also went nice and relaxed. A Movie, I called my brother in Italy, my parents visit, my sister and her friend visiting. A Tasty snack and a drink. Eating together. That's how my first weekend flew by.

"Es gibt Schnee!" Wijk aan Zee 01-03-2015 20: 01h.

That way you are still a recreational person and that is how you race as a revalidated. I First presented the problems of my leg length difference at the shoemaker. Fortunately, they can increase the slippers and the bath slippers. So now for the first time, but with two different slippers, I tried to get into the pool. Up to a kind of bridge, the walkway, I ride my wheelchair. I thought it was okay if I was helped well to put myself on my left leg, that I am strong enough to hold the fence. With bridge and all of it they then lower me to the desired height or low. I believe it can be 2 meters deep. But I lowered myself quite deeply, because the water is so nice and warm, 34oC. It was just wonderful to experience that I now had absolutely no pain in the water whether I walked forwards, backwards or sideways. This experience made me so happy that my thoughts wandered happily to a lot of adventure. One of the sportsmen, who has known me for years, shouted across the side: "Are you all right Han?" It was clear that I could see it and I said it was a difference between day and night. Speaking of the pain then, not the difference in water or above water. Yes, that is also a big difference.

The recreational of these days is that a lot of snow has fallen outside. Now that Luigi is just over a week back with me, I am suddenly on winter sports. Here in the dunes it looks beautiful. There are hikers who go out with cross-country poles. If it continues like this you can also get the slats for the day. And I? I'm not afraid of anything. Slipping nicely with the wheelchair. A dog with me who is completely crazy and makes headlines in the snow every few meters. Awesome. What I also looked forward to this afternoon is the person who has already received many descriptions from me. A few minutes before the start I got a cell phone signal that he was driving into the village by now. From that I concluded that he might also like to be welcomed with open arms. Given that I would prefer to do that literally because I feel so much extra energy, but unfortunately that is actually not possible myself, I had Luigi ensure the large reception. I had already chased him a bit. Luigi recognized him immediately and was already barking and wagging my right hand, extension, remote control. Just as pleasant right? Especially if you also love dogs. He must understand the gesture. That I sometimes have my own approach or methods or communication. The acceptance of that, as it is, has sometimes disappointed me very much with friends/men. That it is such a nice friendship now gives me a valuable feeling and therefore also extra energy. But I also receive a lot, I feel that. So, to report a new progress: walked 26 m.

Love pushing the boundaries Wijk aan Zee 08-03-2015 14: 26h.

If I sit in my wheelchair so well and really have no pain at all, I sometimes think I can get out of my wheelchair like that. Then I would like to get up and walk away at such a moment. And then I notice that I want too much at the same time too quickly. But I had a bit of a problem with having to wait half an hour to get my jacket off at home. On the other hand, another reason to practice even harder and to experiment how I would be able to do it safely. With that thick snow, however, they did have exhaust service, so I thought that was good again. Yet I wanted to go out, despite the snow and during the day there are enough people on the street to free me if I got stuck. And I got stuck of course. Two nice Belgian ladies pulled me away again. Because of their accent and the atmosphere of the snowy environment, I just got the feeling that I was a tourist and so were they. "Tasty Glühwein?", I said with a wink. They found that too early. Maybe I should also take that seriously.

It was a better idea to have a cup of coffee at the bakery and do my report there, because they want to know how things are going with me. Then some groceries to catch a glimpse of a certain person, who may already be better known by some than I think, but with a view to privacy I stay pretty vague. Through shopping and chatting here and there, the time went nice and fast. I came up with a truck at home to take off my jacket with Luigi and take it off. Because my wheelchair cushion has now been made somewhat higher and my kitchen stool last weekend, I can now come forward myself. I just cannot get up like I used to. Without aids or imprints, but straight through stretching my legs. Now I place the wheelchair as close as possible to the table so that the right armrest rests on it. Then I support with my right arm that has just enough strength to push me on that armrest and I also continue to support while standing and shuffling towards the kitchen stool. Then I am happy that I will sit down again. If I am standing sideways next to the table, leaning on the table, and I bend down a little, which I also find scary, then Luigi pulls off my coat. Then I sit down again and shake my shoulders to lower my sleeves. If it gets stuck, then Luigi pulls the sleeve. All in all it may seem like half an hour, but I think it took 5 minutes. The most important thing is that it works.

What also went unnoticed and while playing was also a very nice exercise, driving a model airplane by simulator on the laptop and connected equipment that my visit had brought with me. It looked so easy, but it was hard! I could not dare it that I could not let the plane land without crashing. It went reasonably well in the air. I even stood in front of it. And so, I trained my leg muscles unnoticed, because in the fire of the game I stand longer than I think. But I finally got the plane on the ground. Drinks earned! I just stick with my own joysticks ... car and wheelchair steering, isn't it?

Humour Velserbroek 12-03-2015 2:53 pm.

Many people in my department have become invalid overnight. A lot of them are getting better, but I notice that there is a certain sense of humour and that is why I feel quite at home in this department, because I also want to keep seeing the sunny side. I don't know any better with my own situation or I deal with it with humour. Of course, I am a serious person. Rehabilitation or cure is indeed serious business. I also have my thoughts and feelings about that. Thoughts about hope for rapid improvement, thoughts about patience what I am yielding, thoughts about love and happiness, thoughts about faith, thoughts about new challenges that I want to take on, thoughts about being somewhat secluded anyway, but that I am happy that every year through 2015 can blow day by day, because blowing is something that just happens at the sea. Given that I now 4x a week in the morning at 8.30 a.m. I am expected to be in the swimming (walk) bath before that time as a bath guest in my bathrobe with bare legs underneath with fashionable black slippers outside in the wind to be able to have Luigi do his first pee otherwise he has to hold it up too long, while most employees just arrive with their necks in the collar and warmly dressed, looking worried and asking if I am cold. Well, you get hard and strong. Afterwards is the warm pool water. I think it's the kick of the temperature difference, just like in the sauna, but then the other way around. I also wanted to give the bathing staff a different start. Once again, I could not resist staying too serious and had a request without ulterior motives. I wanted the trainer to lower the walkway to its end point, incidentally it seems to be 1.60 m, which is about my height, with me on it. With the idea it was already double, so I also got the weak smile. I could hold my breath long enough if the bridge did not want to go up, where the chance was very small. And so, I slowly came down under water. Behind me I heard him laughing all the time until I was upstairs again. I no longer had it all above water level.

In the ward it was also fun that morning: "Like Hanneke, here's your stuff and your shot." They should know once, history now, ... other times. The shot, in this case blood thinner in syringe form, was for the last time. "Ahhh, can I do it myself, the last one?" "Only now", does the nurse says "she can do it herself! A week extra." cried the sister. And with my crooked fingers I professionally hack the syringe in my belly, press it out slowly and pull it out at a nice speed. "Please sister, I have something for you." With some disbelief and wonder, she tackles the syringe. I had fun. And in this way life is not difficult or boring and I can handle my disability just like that.

'Love Is All' Wijk aan Zee 17-03-2015 16: 47h.

Rehabilitation is actually often very well thought about yourself. Thinking about how your options were before and whether you can achieve them again. Preferably, of course, a bit more and better. When I ask myself why I always want to go to extremes, it is to get my drive and everything I have and what I am out of it. But not always only for myself, which can also give me satisfaction, but also for those around me. What I can draw even more strength from and what I want to do a little extra for is someone who has come on my life path who lets me know and feel that I am not just someone. That I can be there and be special. A very nice experience from which I hope to gain a lot of strength, because I am not there yet, my condition is really not on track. But what is nicer than that people want to put so much energy into you to lend a heart to you. Play with the dog and then run after the ball, because the dog changes his mind. That one day I receive a musical card from which the music of my own choir suddenly comes. All that effort to be able to sing on one card with 60 to 70 men (sorry, woman) for me! It was clear to me that they already had fun with it. One evening I came back here and got a singlet "love is all" from that singing frog from a fellow rehabilitation person. Gosh, how appropriate I found this. My frog story was probably going to do the rounds. I've been saving them for years. It started with a frog carrying a sign with the text: "you have a lot of kisses to get your prince." So, I keep saving and kissing frogs, but no prince on the white horse. They are stuck on impossible horses. Have you ever tried a thoroughbred Arabian? I See many galloping past. Now I lunge a beautiful specimen within an acceptable radius that I want to hold on for as long as possible to get used to me and that I give free rein. The more laps I complete with my prince on horseback, the dizzier I get and I finally bite.

Hospital visit VUMC 27-03-2015 15: 19h.

Today I had to come back for a check-up at the orthopaedist in the VUMC. Always a bit exciting and I knew that it would be a long afternoon again. Also, because I often have to wait. I don't drive myself yet. I am glad that the walking is already a bit better. And today I wanted to ask if I could already make the 'boarding movement'. To ease the tension away from me a little, I chose my outfit with the nursing care for today with some humour. I thought it would be nice, since I had to appear with the 'Belgian Moroccan' who was short in stature, to put on leggings with red, black and grey striped stripes. That shows even longer? With that 3 cm longer, I already feel so grown. Who knows I might just stand in front of him. Luigi also received some attention before we leave. His guide harness was first thoroughly cleaned. It is nevertheless an honour to be allowed to enter the hospital with a dog. Then you have to look neat. Unfortunately, we had to wait for the bus for the outward journey. At the X-ray waiting room I was the only one. The other waiting room that was there was already full. To be honest, I thought the air conditioning was a bit too much. I sat there pacing, but since I was sitting alone, I did some leg exercises. Once it was our turn, it seemed as if Luigi had to undergo [hence we] so nervously he did. He jumped up and down with the front legs three times to give me a rubber. He had to go behind the screen for the radiation. Then we moved to the doctors' next waiting room. It looked like a creche there. But the children were very happy that there was a dog. The doctor who finally operated on me, the Nigerian [Eddy Murphy] spoke to me twice with a friendly smile, interested in what was going on in the waiting room, and asked if I wasn't too bothered by my leg length difference. I said that there were still a lot of things involved, but that it can all be solved. The doctor with whom I had the consultation was also very satisfied. In principle I can do everything with some caution. According to him, I was my own specialist and he left it to me to try things, because I am not a standard case. After the conversation I had a friendly request if he would send the digital X-ray to my email address one of these days. I already had it the next morning.

The return trip was also very long. Waiting for the bus to arrive, then picking up another patient who was also the first to be brought home to another hospital, who had been stuck in traffic. That's why I now know for sure again ... try again quickly in my own car.

At Rehabilitation Centre I had been dropped off. I took a breath for a while now and probably Luigi too. First as close as possible to the beach and recover from a mild temperature, the sound of waves, shrieking seagulls, a mad dog and almost setting sun. What else do you want? Cup of coffee?

Cookie with it? Velserbroek 01-04-2015 19: 02h.
There were some rumours that a date of dismissal had already been set, without anybody having consulted with me like that. During the patient discussion I therefore explained that I can shuffle a few meters with a stick, but that I do not yet see myself walking with boiling hot pans and I see myself bending over with my mouth above the hot plates. I am not stable at all, especially when I get tired. So last weekend I thought I'd start training hard. Leave my crutches at Rehabilitation Centre and only take the walking stick. At home I managed to put back my office chair that was temporarily put away to make room for the wheelchair behind the PC itself. I Prepared the necessary cups of tea or Wiener Melange myself. But still I came across myself sometimes and not just in the mirror. And only an empty plate and dish, army could not because the cat had licked it as good as clean, and put some cutlery in the sink to put under water and then some rags with a damp cloth was very tiring. And I cannot train harder. Even when I had to go to the toilet, I started walking from the living room. In between the companies constantly trying to keep my legs moving. Even while watching television. Just as well at Rehabilitation Centre.

They should know! It is difficult for me to always call someone in: "Look!" It reminds me of that advertisement of that woman who asks her husband at every moment of the day: "Cookie with it?" When I am standing on the wall rack just before myself: "Training there?" When I stand at the foot of my bed practicing steps "training there?" If I exhaust Luigi and meanwhile alternate one leg by keeping the other leg stretched out as long as possible. And even when I'm in bed I do abdominal exercises with the chin on my chest. "Training there?" That is quite tiring and it may seem exaggerated, but I felt pressured. Even if a big question mark was put at 'dismissal' symbolically, the feeling with me did not go away. I seem to be so positive in my daily life, which is just a nice thing most of the time, but now I also gave the impression that I can handle it all at home. But even then, I find it difficult to accept that without my opinion decisions will go around that I cannot handle at all. I suffered a relapse, particularly mentally. No matter how much I would like to go home, no matter how well I try. It should not be a race against the clock. It would be such a shame if something happened. Okay I like challenges, but I also know when I can take them and when I run too much risk. I have to be patient, but now I have to transfer it to the supervisors. Otherwise I really feel rushed.

This week I went into the 'pub' to celebrate the last day of a rehab together with a nice cold Hoegaarden beer or two. That was calling the night nurse at night, who was already informed, because I came back quite late. "What is that?" she asked. Fortunately, she took it nicely.

If you are always dependent on others, doctors, care providers, family, friends, I tend to take this into account verbally and in my attitude. Also, a form of courtesy. I have noticed often enough that you sometimes have to stand on your stripes and even that I want to continue to do politely. It has just crept in, throughout my life, that I am strong, open, cheerful and challenging in character. But I still occasionally lack the communication to send signals of sadness, discontent or powerlessness and assertiveness. I think that is also the reason why I also like to communicate in a different way. Music, singing, poetry and painting of course. Whether or not immediate hearing can be indicated there and whether I can do something with it when I need it is not so in this case now. I am in other circumstances that I am not used to. Less privacy. And a lot of information, incentives that come to me through different people, which will feel that they are hindering my rehabilitation due to the unconscious pressure that is exerted instead of the opportunity to give me the time and space to recover and my own explanation. To be able to give. It will lead a life of its own if I cannot express myself. I first had to get a push from a friend to express my feelings. It turned out that after I had talked with the rehabilitation doctor, social worker and 'my responsible nurse' things were not right and the misunderstandings started running with me. Yet I could not let go of it completely. To put myself on different thoughts, I sometimes numb them with stuff, but then there is more danger lurking.

First a cup of coffee at home on the terrace at the bakery. My report on the steps forward of course and my training to save me a little at home. They thought along and from now on I am allowed to make a call, then my bread per two cuts in bags is ready for the freezer. If that is not a service! Then I spoiled myself at the hairdresser. New look. Immediately afterwards I show this look to a special friend for me to feel better. There is now less opportunity to come by spontaneously, which I quite miss. After a conversation outside at his car to evaluate my week to him, our roads broke up again. I did not like the return trip to Rehabilitation Centre which now has to be done by volunteer transport. I was not detained and other people had to be picked up. I long for freedom, independence, being on the road again, sitting alone in my car with my own thoughts and music and dog. Hours of driving without getting tired. The rescue came. One evening I was called to go through the final details for the 'tomorrow' lecture. This was the only lecture I could not cancel because I had no telephone number. It was honestly called. Now I have to arrange transportation. I Called a retired volunteer whom I have known for years before I had my own car and who drives me when it is needed or who drives with me when I want to drive myself, but also need assistance. He found it surprising of course, he had time and a bus. I went there the following afternoon. Through my house to pick up my reading gear to Aalsmeer where I had a wonderful afternoon. My waterfall of words fortunately did not tire the people, but fascinated them very much. It also seemed like I wanted to make up for the damage. I felt so good. This life was known to me. Telling about my adventures, my experience of life and the drive for art. I had a good taste again. Aalsmeer and flowers also cannot do without. I received a beautiful bunch of roses, fresh from the greenhouse. They are from the night greenhouse and when I close my eyes in the evening, I smell the rose scent and I feel an incentive to go on an adventure again.

There is music in it   Velserbroek 16-04-2015 18: 47h.

We are a bit behind, because the PC at Rehabilitation Centre does not have an internet connection at the moment. My program for the entire week is becoming more extensive. If I blow up the dust, it is now also due to all the movement, energy, racing through the building and Luigi that leaves its fur here and there. I think he's getting a summer coat. To be honest, I now hope to communicate better with my practitioners. I myself will have to take the initiative for that which I still find difficult. Because all those small advances that I see myself I cannot share with anyone emotionally. Of course, I still do it for myself, but I would like to share and evaluate it much more with someone. Someone who fights with me. In my independent exercises that also happen in exercise rooms, I sometimes get so absorbed that I lose everything around me, but I can go on for so long. I miss feedback, but then I suddenly hear a concerned rehab in the doorway: "Hanneke, you have been busy for a long time!" Pull down four kilos of weights with both arms per second for fifteen minutes. That is around 900 times. I Hold onto the wall rack forwards and backwards or sideways, to which another rehab responds: "I get tired when I look at it. Girl, I admire you a lot. You work hard." Then I almost shoot full and sometimes I shoot full, but then with laughter. They are cheerful notes that I can use. More than physical recovery is needed. Mentally I also need a kick. My self-confidence is slightly less. That way I cannot lose my frustration in this institution. I want more, my life and adventures again. It is up to me to visit them. It is my honour to hold the reins. Creating situations in which I start to feel good. I bought a new pan flute and initiated it in a church service from the Rehabilitation Centre with a mini-concert. A song solo and a song accompanied by music via a CD. I will do this more for the time being. Nice for the listeners and nice to express my feelings. That same week, now in consultation with 'my' nurse, I booked two lectures as part of my recovery to get some more out of it. For me the opportunity to share a piece of story and vision through my art. Carrying out a piece of life with serious subjects, but dressed in a dose of humour, where it is taken seriously.

The end of my week gave more beautiful music and happy notes. Someone I think and know myself, who makes an effort to get inside me. Who wants to look through my eyes and is fascinated by that. It fascinates me too. The knowledge that this person grants me so much, very much, that my self-esteem becomes even stronger. And who, consciously or unconsciously, has given so many cheerful notes. Pain or no pain. Fight or no fight. Dependence or no dependence. Experience or compassion. I feel a lot. And if one day my 'freedom' is given back to me, I cannot express how fantastic that is. No more cars for three months. For quite some time I have always thought about fitting and measuring through those 3 cm longer leg and had the necessary care. A number of hours was spent by that person tuning the distances in my car from the seat and the joystick to me. This has to do with automatic locking / unlocking of the seat with which the switching is activated or deactivated. Protection against theft, but a bit complicated in an emergency or now in this case with a new adjustment. A Bit technical. I watched this struggling, tinkering friend attentively and listened to all the explanations of his actions. I thought it was all so exciting whether theory and practice would be right. The feeling of being in the car and being able to leave again. So much uncertainty passed through me for a moment whether my constitution could handle it all. But it surprises me time and again that the calm, charisma and patience with which he works, he calms me in my head and I am confident that things are going well. Ready for a first test drive! My girlfriend, who was staying for a weekend, had also arrived. She thought it was a safe idea that I set off with Pierre 'the mechanic'. This soon turned out to be the case, because the joystick was barely moving for me. At the first roundabout we have returned and went everything wrong using the joystick. Pierre did not find it difficult, but hey, I cannot stand such a hard worker. The joystick turned out to be too tight. Of course, with a view to safety, but here the weather works slightly differently. Fastened the joystick on the spot. Test drive two! Getting in and out might go a bit stiff, but really no more pain, nowhere. Awesome! I get air again. I no longer feel trapped. Now I can become myself and me again and meet my freedom. Go and stand when I want and can. There is enough left where I need help, but transporting myself at great distances has also given my life form and content. I have been able to build up so much that such a substance cannot be taken from me. It was such a relief that it was done in one afternoon. Nice cheerful notes on my path.

Sportswoman Velserbroek 24-04-2015 18: 36h.

I was a bit surprised by all the small changes that my 'long' leg had brought about lately. Not so much that it was an operated leg. That fact actually wears out a bit. The pain is gone and the condition is getting better. But what do you want! Walk with physiotherapy, walk with occupational therapy, cookery club with a strict schedule of rest and action to prepare some meals. This way I can stand longer and longer and I practice walking and using my energy efficiently. This method seems to be used in sport to perform even better. Recently I even cycle, which I haven't done in 25 years, on an exercise bike with a smaller turn. This also stimulates the circulation of the muscles better and I also feel sporty. When I see the device unmanned, I sometimes go after it myself. I sit with my wheelchair behind it and my feet go into special molds. It is a wonderful feeling.

What also boosted my self-confidence is my red car. Okay, it's not all going smoothly, but it's going again and I think that's really great. And why would you practice small pieces? So again, I am not the person for that. With my father I made a trip to Jaarbeurs in Utrecht planned to sing all day 'the Big sing'. I Got up early. Nicely on schedule. However, the wheelchair had not been in the car yet and I had forgotten all the other dimensions. The handles were always locked in the safety net and the flap could not close.

Then it just broke loose. My father became a little nervous and lifted the chair with the lift way too high so that the fuse burned out. A 40-amp fuse that is only used for large transport and not for passenger cars. Where did I find them again? At the coat rack? There was one, but the elevator did not respond. Also, a bit sure. Wallet? Yes, luckily the lift did it again. Pooh, what a start. Well, cracks with that bin! And nice that it tore. Like a train. Nice car that Kadett. Accelerating, which I do with the left foot, was only very difficult because of the enormous platform sole. I hardly got any movement in that foot. On the way back I got a bit stressed when we had to refuel. When my father was ready and wanted to pay, he first signalled that someone else was standing behind me. I saw that in my rear-view mirror. "Yes, please wait," I thought. "My leg doesn't want to be like that." And for the time being it really didn't want to. Fortunately, my lively imagination ran wild at the time and I started to get involved in the other. "How strange is that lady in front of me, is it going to go well? There is an invalid sticker on the back. Oh, and it also says that I have to keep 3 meters away, because the elevator folds out." I see the car driving a bit backwards. "Well, don't be afraid, the elevator won't open now," I think. And my father, who did not remember the number of the tank, but the amount, was told: "Oh you are driving an Opel Kadett?" To which my father would have thought: "Is she still there?" I explained that the switch went a bit bad. But I had a lot of fun with all that thinking for others. Eaten a sandwich on the parking lot and drank something. Windows nice and open. Freedom, enjoy. We will continue to train in the coming days and otherwise I will look at the 'magic man' again very kindly to come to a better solution together for the foot.

Special guest Velserbroek 06-05-2015 16: 56h.

There are so many forms of freedom. Freedom of expression, freedom of the press, liberation day and in many cases, it means free to go and stand, like a fish in the water, like a bird in the sky, mobility, independence. There are always times when I really cannot avoid being dependent, but as long as I am aware that I can never really be completely free, I keep looking for freedom in so many ways. In addition, I also discovered that it does not go as naturally as you want. That you even have to fight for it. I have experienced oppression. Pain to overcome and combat. For facilities fight until the courtroom. But to always be able to be cheerful in life is because I also experience my life as special and that also makes an impression on others. Two years ago, I was already in Rehabilitation Centre and suddenly I got my driving instructor on my cell phone. He briefly refreshed my memory and asked if I could remember the day when I was the very first disabled person to ride the joystick. It was an experimental car, I remember, so it contained only a joystick and not, like my car, a steering wheel [for emergency] and a joystick. At that time, I had already been very enthusiastic about my moped, which I also operated with my legs in terms of gas and brakes just like in a car. The fact that I had road experience gave them the deciding factor that I was allowed to do a test drive. The CBR adjustments department was sitting in the back with a large photo camera in their hands. This experience was reported in the CBR magazine. To be able to keep a long story short, this designer of this joystick now retired and remembered that ride as yesterday. The breakdown of the joystick in the service package. The breakthrough that I fought for. So at least worth an invitation, in his opinion, to invite me too, said the driving instructor. I said that I was in a rehabilitation centre because of my hip, but that I would come there anyway, and preferably by car. I Made a small painting in Rehabilitation Centre for the honour of being a guest at his farewell party at the CBR (central driving skills) office. His confidence in me at that time did well determine my future. Because of that car I have been able to build a great life.

And now I am in Rehabilitation centre again. Just diligently cycling when my cell phone suddenly rang. Whether I could get away for a few hours in the afternoon to get to the retired volunteer of the bus transport as surprise, because he would receive a 'ribbon'. He had talked about me so many times that I just belonged. Yes, you will end up somewhere else. At the bottom of the basement of a restaurant this time. Since his wife knew that I can chat nicely, she asked me if I wanted to say a word. There were several people saying a word, so I had some time to think. I felt honoured to be so involved with it. In my way I told about my independence and the car and the adventures that I always want to let go. That when the car doesn't work or I don't, people like this man are indispensable. And if he is no longer allowed to drive the bus, after 70 years old, that I want to try to drive myself and possibly, take him away. They laughed at that. But I also tried to make clear the essence of my story, that as long as that remains possible, I go on my own independently and therefore experience many special things.

African Dance Velserbroek 16-05-2015 00: 57h.

It had regularly happened at the dining table of the Rehabilitation Centre that I had a telephone conversation for the umpteenth appointment somewhere in the country. My table companions were not only curious but also very enthusiastic. So enthusiastic that a fairly new modest rehabilitation specialist wanted to raise his voice to give me the floor while eating, so that I could announce that I would also give a lecture especially for the department. Crazy right? Before that I had made nice registration lists to check whether there would be enough interest. The activity supervisor of our department would assist me extra in the evening and I also provided all kinds of goodies for coffee. It really became a nice full room and it became very hot. Afterwards a lot of fun for the bite of lottery tickets that took in Luigi, an ex-revalidated had won my painting. Even afterwards acquaintances came to me whose man is African and was very impressed with both my story and my personal attitude. In his opinion, I was an example of perseverance, especially for Africans with a disability. He was working on a special project. My mind naturally wandered to other places. He would come back to it anyway. A few days ago, I was talking to the neighbour when the phone rang. It was The African brother. The story with the neighbour was stopped, something was waiting for me. Quickly out of the wheelchair, I called for help in the toilet, straight for a little litterbox and then it happened ... my head was not there ... doormat behind me. My foot got stuck and I took everything I came across in my fall along the way. Expiration ... 112 ... strained knee straps, bed rest. No African dance ... step back ...

Velserbroek businesswoman 21-05-2015 16: 39h.

How fortunate that I had first made a 'toilet-call' for assistance and the front door wide open, because Luigi was in all states, but 'alarm' that I once taught him didn't happen. He was so shocked that he just wanted to stay with me and licked me off and ran barking in and out. The toilet assistant of course found me lying between the cat poles and litter box and immediately called her colleague. Bold as I was, I said I would soon have visitors. Someone from Nigeria and if I might not be able to get up. But she only had to half lift my back or a terrible pain screamed through my knee. Then just wait half an hour after calling 112. Well the visitor came to the hospital. I was curious about what my visitor had come for and I needed to have some distraction, and since we just couldn't reverse the situation, I wanted to do business, even though it was between the curtains of the E.R. The situation I was in and the optimism to just keep on was making him laughable African, which also made me a little happier. He had an envelope with a DVD of a project that he is starting up for Africans all over the world. The envelope also contained typical African jewellery for me and the question was whether I wanted to become the ambassador of this project Loversglobal Humanity. I read, I read in the letter, ambition, prestige and a sense of charity. I would be the right person. Yes, you fall steeply backwards. "Oh sister, the right spirit." And that nice smile again. I would of course think about it, but I saw a big challenge in it.

In pain all day in bed. Despite Wiener Melange with Tia Maria and a warm friend at the bed, not a wink. I was allowed to borrow the laptop the next day to mess around on my site and to chat and because it was a laptop of someone else, I naturally also had different music via the Media Player. Not a bad choice by the way. But I enjoyed myself so much. When my parents saw me lying like that, they looked strange. "Does all that sound come from that thing?" my father asked. "Do you actually have pain?" No, I need some attention, I thought. And I got a kiss.

My girlfriend who has had a modified bus for a year and a half would drive me back to the Rehabilitation Centre. After all, we have the same condition, a muscle disease so we know what we can do to each other and she can also estimate my pain very well. It was quite a struggle with a lot of moans and support to get into my wheelchair. I really couldn't strain the leg. It was ten times worse than after my hip surgery. Inside I felt a deep disappointment and powerlessness. I was already there. Why? That's life, I'm afraid.

Experiences Velserbroek 03-06-2015 19: 04h.

The weeks before I fell hardly described my rehabilitation. My head was already preparing for discharge until I fell. For yourself you always try to find answers to difficult situations, the 'why'. But you cannot figure it out. For me it means being called back. Maybe I walked too much beside my shoes. It makes me aware who and what I am. It forces me to have to confront myself. Fighting, fighting. No victory without a fight. I have therefore cut the knot to become the ambassador of Lovers global Humanity to convey my feelings of struggle to my loved ones. When I can mean something for another, another across borders, who or what stops me? Such an injured rot knee? As long as I know that it will pass again and I don't have to live in continuous intense pain, I will continue to use my art across borders.

No one had any idea what was actually going on after I fell. The neighbour next door, I heard later, thought that I had become 'not good', because he only saw me lying dead in the doorway. But anyway, I cannot start anything when I'm lying on the floor. The upstairs neighbour only saw ambulance staff waiting, waiting outside at the folding doors of the car. The worker who was diligently housekeeping did not hear the bell when I was brought back. As the neighbour is also a choir member and told this to another choir member, she too tilted and emailed me again that she had immediately dived into this blog to read what had happened anyway. Everyone experiences it in their own way. Some are impulsive, others withdraw. Confrontation? It would be a shame. I remain who I am. It is not an obligation to walk with me in my life. And if you walk along it will certainly not be a standard walk with difficult moments, I realize that, but who says it should be experienced that way? I will never let the suffering prevail, but 'dearly'. Whoever can share joys and sorrows with me, will eventually receive love, not sorrow. No routine, but adventure. No surface, but depth. Now or never. Now or ever. Sorry, I think I go for a bit. I just need fellow walkers. Walking can sometimes be so difficult and then you can give any luggage to others. Or if other walkers have a heavy load, I want to wear it.

Art with disabled children Velserbroek 03-06-2015 22: 27h.

A few weeks ago I was invited by the VSN Netherlands Muscle Diseases Association to participate in the Kids day. A day for children aged 4-12 with or without muscle disease. There were all kinds of introductory activities with live music not only for the kids but also very suitable for the parents. My workshop involved giving 6 x 15 children mouth painting lessons. That seemed so great to me that I really didn't want to cancel this activity despite my painful knee. My girlfriend would ride me in her modified bus. Both therefore called in very early to get dressed. To be sure I was sitting backwards in her bus, if she had to make an emergency stop. I was too scared of my leg. It was a wonderful hot day against the tropical. We were really out of it. Everything was arranged perfectly on location. We were able to park the bus nicely in the shade. All supplies such as paint, pallets, brushes, cups and place mats were present. I feel very much at home as a teacher. In a nice way I explained what the intention was and of course I showed it what made a big impression on my pupils between 8-12 years old.

Children are so open, easy and straightforward. While working they tell everything about their illness. That made me want to give them even more pleasure and some attention. They did their best for me. And that it made an impression I heard later from the parents.

During the break there was plenty to eat and drink and I had two hours off. In that time, we could go for a nice walk with the dogs. After all, it was a wooded area. That way I could breath for the next round.

At the end of the day, my room was full of paintings. Magnificent. They were able to pick up everything including materials before departure and I was allowed to pick out their own card or bookmark. All the children thanked me and hoped to see me again maybe next year. I received a painting as a reminder from one student. Tired but very satisfied, I was sitting backwards behind my girlfriend in the bus while my thoughts were dreamily passing through.

What is freedom? Wijk aan Zee 29-06-2015 8:45 pm.

Once I have heard the children of the 'kids day', from which so much has been taken over the years, and when I look around me here in the rehabilitation centre and see that whole members have decreased, I realize that such the fallback of my fall is of a temporary nature. It is very disappointing after all the training and energy that I had put into it, that I started practically from the beginning and had to endure a lot of pain during the first weeks. Then you are much more vulnerable and I have to guard my limits very clearly for myself. Up to my pain threshold and my physical possibilities at that time. It hurts me twice if that is not understood and executed. My emotional boundary is therefore ignored. If I then stand up for myself, it is a form of assertiveness that I simply cannot do anything to myself. People sometimes think differently about this. When you have been dependent all your life, your attitude has become a piece of life protection. Before you know it, it will be decided for you whether you will even be used. That is why I just want to keep a good eye on my limits. I became irritable and restless because of it, even depressed, but I have no other way of dealing with this situation. It was all sorts of concerns that kept me busy, but especially my physical condition that ran backwards in rapid speed.

In order not to worry, I always want to leave. A lecture was also open in the city Moordrecht. This time my brother from Nigeria wanted to join because of the project for Africa to make PR by also filming my presentation and broadcasting it in Africa. A lecture with a special accent. I enjoyed telling about our meeting and why we decided to become an ambassadors for Lovers global Humanity wherever it will lead.

A while later I also stood at an art market in a city Breukelen and brought Pierre from especially for that occasion to let me help for a few days, because I still can't get up myself. Then a few days of help is nice. We even tried to get back in the car. It was a bit too early and it still hurt a lot, but once I sat down, I might as well have started driving. To Alkmaar! Spontaneously visit a friend, a walk with the dogs and on the way back delicious fries in the car. This freedom is so important to me, I will continue to fight for it, which I have been doing for 4 years.

Last auctions Velserbroek 09-07-2015 17: 01h.

Unfortunately, I have regularly found that there is very little communication when it comes to changes in treatment or medication. Internal communications that are important to patients, so not only do I notice, are never passed on. It has always been talked about afterwards. I cannot imagine that it is up to me, because I have great adaptability. The fact that I should have an extra consultation with the social worker for this, tells me that they do not have the capacity to adapt if someone deviates somewhat from the protocol. I may be someone with a bit of instructions, but it is not that extreme either. Now I can be bothered by that, but that doesn't help, so I opt for a different strategy. Put energy in moving forward. In between therapies, you can work on 'fitness' again. Increase the pace and be ahead of the rest of the practitioners. What I should be able to do next week, I can do tomorrow, of course I will keep that to myself. If I can only be in charge of myself, I feel much stronger. Then I come across myself once in a while, now I continue. I want to get away from struggles, memories, sorrows and sorrows of others and myself. I want my own world and friends back. For others I want to be there again. It's been nice. And if it becomes difficult? A hot tub has been reserved at home at the aid station for a couple of weeks, where I can relax for at least an hour in the evening. Sometimes with coffee and sometimes with coffee and liqueur. After that I feel great and listen to music at home and I am sitting at the PC. I don't really have that much inspiration for painting. I have, however, completed an assignment; a portrait of a former rehab, sold!

Fortunately, I am getting out of my wheelchair again, which I keep to myself, although it still hurts. This week I abandoned the brace as much as possible. I have arranged the bedside table at Rehabilitation Centre while standing. If there was nobody in the gym, I went to work there. At home I brush my teeth while standing. I get up several times to be able to access something and then take the opportunity to stand a little longer. A few times a day, at home, I try to walk at least 15 minutes with my walking stick and ... I have driven a car again. This time I could get in the car with the housekeeper [and my brace]. A fellow who just cycled past wanted to ride with me as a co-driver. A tourist ride made while chatting, practiced with a lot of cornering and therefore also the legs, through a beautiful environment. The end is near. I like to hold the reins [and the joystick]. They must be surprised that I have my own dismissal date. But it is not over yet that beautiful summer.

Final Countdown Velserbroek 23-07-2015 12: 59h.

This week another space shuttle will be launched from NASA. Hopefully with a happy ending. I also count the days myself. I had already booked my vacation this spring and I thought I could get away from it for a while. then to continue my rehabilitation, but the room MUST be free. I was working there anyway not to stay much longer. You do keep some telephone contact with friends or via skype or facetime, but it makes me feel a bit lonelier. You stick to your program and put your mind to rehabilitation, but your feeling wants more. Then a dune-walk with Luigi makes me think. When I end up on the beach where the wind is blowing in my ears, I get a breath of fresh air and wonder about surfing with a skydiver or something. A kid who is fighting the sea with his kite and a surfboard. I can look at it for a long time and dream how it might feel. Some seek the battle with the forces of nature. Others are surprised by forces of nature. Life is also full of surprises and fights. Sometimes you look for them yourself, sometimes it suddenly happens to you and you are left empty-handed. I was able to prepare for some fights like the operation, but my fall was a fight that was not planned. And just about my car, that's what I'm fighting for. And so, I think there are people who do battle every day, even with themselves. But I have stood the fire through all the battles. "Never give up what you are fighting for!" There is always a moment in a day with something valuable that you can use to create strength that you have created yourself or that will come your way. My rehabilitation period is over. Ups and downs, but goals are there to be achieved. I have had to deal with many rehabilitators and we learned from each other. I also hope that by deviating somewhat from the protocol, I was unable to relocate or overcome a bit of uneasiness and insecurity among the care providers. For them I had made my own card with an appropriate text for each one separately. And because I became a little 'African minded' I played a song on my pan flute at the end of the church service with the CD of 'The Lion King' in which the African genre can be heard beautifully. The title was 'poor land' after the original song 'shadow land'. Strangely enough I couldn't sleep the last night in Rehabilitation Centre.

The next morning at home early again for the big drive to the adjustment garage in 's Hertogenbosch, still to screen all adjustments. The lock that lets the seat stop to the rear position, to get in and out, could even be placed slightly backwards, so that I now believe I am almost really sitting in the back seat, but with my new leg length it went in - and getting out so difficult that I am happy with this adaption now. When accelerating remains very difficult with that thick platform sole, they may want to move the touch switch. If it really is no longer possible, even go to the headrest. Can you see it? Switch with the head. The joystick and the locking mechanism of the front seat to be able to reach the joystick just right, which 'my' technical greengrocer has adjusted, were also fully approved. A Surprise was that, since it is no longer a 'company car', but a private individual, I had to pay cash. They hadn't said that! Pin, pin, pin, pin ... It belongs to me and as long as it drives, I drive, I am an ARTIST and I am free. Oh ... how good I rode that day and I am happy that every day that is independent is another day extra.

Chapter 2

But more happened with those beautiful blue eyes and long blond curls. Unfortunately, my gentle nature preys on gentlemen who wanted more than once for themselves. That my body did not function as I would like, oh well I was at peace with that, but that my lively, happy mind was so hurt by unwanted behaviour, also intimately I had a lot of trouble with that. It made me really sad how I was and how I wanted to be, a happy blond girl. But I didn't dare to be anymore. I could not be like that anymore, because if my thoughts even went a bit in that direction of dependence, the fear caught my throat. I got a huge dislike for that dependence I simply had to be exposed to every day, whether I wanted to or not. Time and again an enormous tidal wave of fear and sorrow surfaced that I could not face. Soothing agents were prescribed by my doctor such as oxazepam and diazepam that I soon could not get enough of and I even developed a physical and mental dependence on them. I focused on the art, the mouth painting. Once I painted, I felt the fear, but luckily, I forgot all the fearful images. When I was in bed again and had to undergo my dependent position for the last time before sleeping the fear and loneliness came. I closed my eyes but time and again I saw everything before me again. Guys who pulled me onto their lap in the pub and grabbed my breasts and guys who kissed drunk on my mouth and even crammed their genitals into my mouth to cum at toilets I thought I was choking on it, so the emotions were now oppressive. I still had an old plastic Rosary that I put in my mouth in bed to slide bead by bead along my tongue to pray holy Mary greetings and Our Fathers. Praying and crying I fell asleep with the beads in my mouth.

I continued to paint and became a member of the Association of Mouth and Foot Painters worldwide. It gave me some peace that God let me walk this way in which I saw fellow members with perseverance in the same situation. Just like me, they had passion and charisma. Painting is a great way to express your feelings. My inner struggle and vision of the world around me became increasingly beautiful on paper and on canvas. I went to visit painting clubs where the others painted with hands. It was all about learning to practice all kinds of techniques. Students who were completely absorbed in their own world were not aware that one would paint next to them with a brush in her mouth. But when they looked around; "Yes of course! You don't want to say that you painted that with your mouth, right?" With a modest laugh with my brush in the right mouth corner, I nodded affirmatively. I continued painting without shame. Passion became art.

Art dairy

Vacation?   Velserbroek 21-08-2015   12: 03h.

The month of August should be the opportunity for me to paint considerably. I recovered nicely from everything and in September the artist life will start again. There will be lectures, exhibitions and who knows what else. I always get surprised, but at least I never say no. However, it is becoming tight again. But performing under pressure can also give a kick. Continue, or start in the evenings when there are no more distractions apart from my own music to get in the right mood. It's dark outside. The lights from the neighbours go out one by one and I am absorbed in my painting. Sometimes it depends on how much I feel about it. With landscapes it is the respect and beauty that fascinates me, with animals it is endearing and with portraits or models it is deeper desires. What I would like, but which can also be elusive. There are those thoughts that I would only like to share with one person who is in my heart. Only my paintings know it. And as long as I don't know the future, it will remain an adventure. There remains a desire. Passion remains there. There remains attraction.

Just bad luck Velserbroek 3-10-2015 5:25 pm.

Every artist will have enthusiasm. Wanting to put down such an urge to work more, want more and get it done. Sometimes at the expense of your own health. Drinks, drugs or other means to keep going. Now I used resources, but that was to forget something very much. My urge to continue is perseverance. That this perseverance is often put to the test is now a certain fact. Just when I think everything runs smoothly again, I can time out again. Now I don't want to start again about rehabilitation, but it comes down to the fact that my shoulder head tore loose due to circumstances. A painful thing at first, because it could not be cast. Fortunately, I still had a brace of my back that I could wrap around my waist with elastic. In this case now including upper arm. It gave great support. The doctor was also satisfied with it. Concernedly, I asked the doctor if the fall could be caused by hip surgery. He said it was just bad luck. So, it did not stop me from getting out of the wheelchair. By the way, what good is it if you no longer have pain in your hips and can walk nicely. I also want to build this walk and improve my condition. Although I do it with extreme caution. There is 12 weeks for the entire healing. After 3 weeks, however, I still wanted to continue with my activities. Luckily, I never use the injured arm while driving, so I drove myself to my holiday destination, lectures and higher court, for the car. I wondered on the spot if it didn't make a big impression that under these circumstances I could move on completely independently. Not. The only thing that got the attention was whether or not I would be in isolation without a car and according to the 'medical data' it was not. Too bad then, just bad luck. At a moment like that you'd better set your mind to zero. I have my car now; I always have my painting gear with me. Also, my pan flute during my vacation. Now let me not lose my joy and share my feelings with fellow holiday makers. An afternoon was spontaneously inserted for me to talk about my work and life. Full of interest I was also asked to show people all my passions to make them happy with my music. And I like to make people happy. Art attracts people to and from each other. Certainly music. I need to process my indefinable feelings and oppressive thoughts. It is my communication at that time. I do isolate without that. It's so nice to offer fellow people something and you get something nice in return. But now I really have to start painting. A castle. I'll get that done today. My schedule is to make 15-20 this year. Night work.

Another wind is blowing Velserbroek 23-01-2016 17: 23h.

Are they dark days, is it the bleak wind, are they unanswered questions, is it unrequited love? At least it was clear to me that things had to change. I wanted to do something I had never done before. Something that would make my adrenaline rise. I had met a trucker from the north through a communication program on the PC. Knowing is perhaps a big word and I didn't want to let myself know at all. I did, however, immediately clarify that there is more to me than what you think you see at first sight. A reference to my site seemed the best. Actually, I was pretty worried that it would be over by then, but the trucker remained curious and perhaps became more fascinated by it. Thus, however, the contact persisted via PC still. Wherever I was. In Limburg or at home. There was clear interest. Have I not fallen into a trap more often? Do I look it up myself again? First, telephone maintenance, so that I could hear his voice. Frisian. Very serious actually. Confusing me. He himself suggested traveling together half to a location for both of us in the middle to Wieringerwerf. I already found this suggestion a gesture to reassure me. Before leaving I sought some distraction again at the bakery and while drinking my cappuccino together with another customer and her dog, fun. She had not sought it after me and did not believe it if someone else had said it. Suddenly a text message came in while laughing. '2 more hours, xxx ?.' He was already counting down. She spontaneously pulled out my mittens so that I could respond, but I could barely see what I was doing through the nerves, so the text probably seemed like a secret code. I'm lk7go0-/ing?, I said. I spent an hour on the road thinking about what I had started, what I would talk about, how I could ask for help, etc. It was a bright day. I needed my sunglasses and a shiny lipstick looked nice. My navigator brings me to my destination, but why at a side entrance? My trucker couldn't find me. Everything but my car opened, door and tailgate. And I had already got out to be on the lookout. He came there. He now stood before me. The trucker? Everything expected, except this petite, discreet and nice guy with his sparkling eyes. He had something for me, he said, and walked back. A nice bouquet for me. A wonderful start to a 'blind date'. As the day progressed I remained so surprised at his outspoken kindness that it really made me happier. Was it so strange to have done this? I do not think so. The last time I was a little bit lived again. Now I had chosen this myself and I enjoyed it a lot and not only myself. This person was so committed to me that I continued to wonder about it. We have been able to tell a lot to each other up to and including the hot meal. That was quite a deal. Once I was back on the road again and dived into the dark of the A7, I spontaneously laughed. What happened to me anyway? When I arrived home, I thought I was in control when I came across Herman Finkers a comic with a nice accent, that I saw everything passing by again. Unbelievable, what a day! I want more with this?

Packing and leaving Velserbroek 06-02-2016 19: 58h.

My paintings will brighten up another location. Through my site I received the invitation to exhibit at a 'MEE' office for six months at least. My work had already been taken off the walls of the previous room where they were hung by my parents who live nearby. That way they could store the paintings with them for a day. I was planning to get up early, but I had slept through my alarm clock. My head was still a bit in Friesland. Get me dressed quickly. Lenses cleaned and of course put in. Spread bread and put it in my bag. To gas station, because there was not enough in the tank. Then on to parents. Luigi had not even been out yet. In the meantime, mother did that. Dad loaded the car with paintings, which took such a long time that mother were coming back. Could she just give me my sandwich. Quickly pour in some pills with some water from the Luigi bottle and all that behind the wheel. Then left for city Gouda at the 'MEE' office. Shall I call the trucker right now? I changed my mind while driving. At a traffic light I managed to press my Bluetooth headset through the headrest to dial his number with voice recognition. He was just in bed after his night shift. The trip went very well. Once at the destination I can do the same with the Bluetooth to get me out of the car. Unfortunately, I also needed a little more help with moving, because my electric wheelchair was broken. Now I still had a folding wheelchair, but I have to be pushed with it. So that was quite a chore. First brought the paintings to safety on the 1st floor. Then I followed and a terribly enthusiastic Luigi who wanted to show he was a great assistance dog. I had earned a cup of coffee and Luigi a bowl of water. We discussed the course of the day and how we could work best. We immediately saw that the canteen also had a nice wall to hang some pen drawings.

The rest, a total of 25, was always per 2. We put them against the wall that we thought they were doing well and I was constantly driven to them for my approval. It went pretty well that way. During the break when the canteen was full, the reactions already came. A painting from Italy was even recognized. where I have been and that person too. We even turned out to have been on the same campsite, but not the same year. So from one conversation came the other. The organizer asked if I would like to come again with friends or acquaintances, or perhaps more often. I just couldn't see everything because of a lack of time. So left satisfied again. This summer probably a nice trip that way.

Super dog Velserbroek 02-03-2016 14: 44h.

My electric wheelchair has been broken for weeks. I thought I could see the rain again. The electrical part turned out to be totally worn out. It could mean that I can request a whole new wheelchair from the municipality. The same municipality that does not consider a replacement car necessary for me and that would now have to fit a new wheelchair that of course would like to be fitted into this car! Fortunately, the engineers have known me for years and they also know how important that car is to me and that it will not help me if I cannot take a wheelchair with me. One of the engineers tried to argue that the old wheelchair should be retained and that a new electric chassis with control had to be ordered. If not, if they wanted to adjust the car on the new wheelchair. "Oh, Mrs. Boot!" they must have thought. In the meantime I had been without my wheelchair for two months and I had a scooter for my own use. But given the duration of the entire process and the fact that the scooter could be used outdoors and I, even though I was tired of it, walked inside everything, tiredness started to bother me. One evening when I was taking Luigi out and I was watching one of my cats, because it wanted to come around for a walk, if necessary, I had my thoughts on the road in a fraction of a second. I was only able to reconstruct what happened on the basis of information that I was told afterwards and what I can remember at times. I myself remember that I was lying in the street and that a woman turned me clockwise on my back with the intention of perhaps addressing me if I wanted to be helped. Since I thought there was nothing wrong with that, I agreed. But soon I saw shocked faces. In the background I saw another person, a man, with a cell phone to call 112. I followed their eyes confusedly, watching the ground to my left in the street. I also automatically looked to the left of me on the street. There was a whole puddle of blood. It seemed wise to me to turn back on my left side. I remember the rest at times. At least I was told that Luigi was barking that way. I was not hit by a car otherwise I was lying on the roundabout clockwise. So a young woman seemed to have responded to the barking. She then looked out the window and saw me lying motionless with a barking dog by my side. This looked so impressive that I think this lady called her parents to look at me.

It's so weird that I cannot remember anything about Luigi. I was quite at a dangerous point. Fortunately it was late and there was hardly any traffic. These people then took the dog and the scooter on my instructions to the aid station where they told their story. I also seem to have said that I could ever walk my whole life when I was asked if I could get up. That is not me, but afterwards comical. But thanks to Luigi, all this help has started. Who knows how long I would have been there differently? And what could not happen if a motorist saw me in the spotlight at the last minute? It all ended well. Five stitches in my head, staples actually, and a week of rest. Time out.

Velserbroek sweeties 27-03-2016 23: 25h.

Most of the presentations I give are for adults; women's associations or senior clubs. Barely recovered from my fall and I just call my duty. But it is so surprising when you sometimes get the impression that because of all the hustle and bustle it seems that beautiful things are coming your way again. It is time that I gave the children attention again. First I was invited to Heliomare to show my work to 4 preschool children with severe spasm. They were helped by the class assistants. And what could be more fun than even being allowed to stand on the table. And when I see those kiddo's, I also understand that despite my crooked hands and dangling everyone loved me because of my naughty head. When I see those cans in the eyes, I want to pick them up. Should I have stood in front of the class?

I like to convey something pedagogical or even to say so. When I just came to live here, it already looked like a cream. Children have an open mind and are curious. As brutal as they can be, they can also listen well when you are engaging with it and you also listen. Again and again; Hanneke! Then I look expectantly at the child and the story comes naturally. I also regularly have two teenagers for a day or two. Guys from two different families who just need something different now and then and are happy to be with me. We go for a walk in the woods, have a drink somewhere or watch a movie and later simply go to the snack bar. And me as a mother feels nice.

I also went to the farm of a second cousin to go to the school of the youngest son. When I was a teenager myself, I always came to stay during the summer vacation in this farm. Now one of the brothers lives in the parental home. I could not resist driving into the yard there. Where has the time gone? 30 years ago, we were driving a cargo bike through the cornfields. I was on the wheel because I couldn't climb it. It went so well and because I was sitting sideways, my long hair blew nicely in the wind and half in my face. Sometimes we also walked through the wheat and chewed some grains. The best thing was to build a secret hut between the potato crates. There we would have a picnic halfway in the dark. That you can think of so much at the same time in such a yard.

It was a lot of fun at the school. After a cup of coffee, which I did not take because it was so hot, all the children of the entire school [58] were waiting in a large circle. They were allowed to ask me anything. In the meantime, I showed how I drank the coffee further and Luigi had a great time with a foam ball that I kept kicking into the circle. How exciting that was. But then the real thing; Mouth painting. Everyone did their best. The little ones backwards on their knees by the chair, the older ones could paint on the table. It has made a great impression. Everyone was allowed to see how I was leaving at the end of the day. Byeeeee!

Running, jumping, flying, diving, falling, getting up and continuing Velserbroek 22-04-2016 20: 18h.

Then I may have lost the lawsuit concerning the car, I am not lost and my research is still continuing. What is on the market now, how can the adjustment garage help, what are the costs now, how do I publicize that I am such an enterprising person and that there is no agency that can help me with a new car? The idea of making a film about it has been a mess for quite some time. Several people have already approached programs for me, but I want to be in control and tell my story my way. Because of my very busy schedule, I had a friend, Pierre, from the south of the country come over who wanted to attend all activities and then record them in all kinds of fragments. First at my adaptation garage in 's Hertogenbosch. The conversation with the chef about the technical details and a short interview. The choral rehearsal, general, together with the great harmony orchestra [of the Circus Jeroen Bosch; Boudewijn de Groot, singer]. One morning, still the same week, I visited and painted a primary school in the neighbourhood. At the same school again present in the evening for 'open house' with illustrations, sales and demonstration. A day later a leisurely boat trip with 'the Sunflower', but even there I am not completely or not at all quiet, because under the short breaks during the bingo, when the drinks went around, I went through the music for the evening performance on the stage. When my elderly table companion asked what I was learning I explained that it was a Tina Turner song, River deep Mountain high, he wanted us to translate it together and the content indeed had deeper thoughts and we were there tasty to smile. And in the evening, I was on stage. And not only that, at night I was in a party centre again to enjoy with my friends. There is no boring day of filming. We always came up with better ideas. Example; you could hardly see the sports steering wheel turning, so when I steer the car with the joystick. White tape was glued on three points to accentuate the rotating steering wheel and you could see how a joystick control works while filming. Another time the sunlight in the car turned out to be annoying again and the background music another time. But that I have a lot of joy and adventure in my life with the car. That was clear to see in the video. And that it would not be my life without my red car!

Chapter 3

The prison seen by a mouth painter

"One day I received a letter from a prison pastor, Jean-Pierre, asking me to make two paintings with flowers. He said that he knew my work from the mouth and foot painters and that it appealed to him. Of course, I like to work on assignment, but then I also want to know more about that person. It became an interesting story that fascinated me. I got a mention of a site about his work as a spiritual caretaker in prison: www. gevangenispastor.nl

This intrigued me even more and my contact with the justice ministry started off in no time. When the paintings were finished, I could have sent it and left it there and thank Pastor Jean-Pierre. But my curiosity and commitment to what happens there continued to draw in such an institution.

A handicap can be somewhat similar to being behind bars.

I then suggested that I be allowed to attend the discussion groups. I wanted to tell about my physical disability, how I feel about life and how I experience my life. I did not know whether it was all possible from an organizational point of view and whether it would entail risks. Pastor Jean-Pierre responded positively to this.

Prisoners are trapped because they have committed mistakes. But I think they are struggling also with problems there that are somewhat similar to mine.

What is feeling trapped?
What is freedom?
How do you deal with being checked by the other person?
when you get a label attached?
How do you live or are you being lived?
Do you think God is still with you?

I wanted to talk about it step by step with the participants. But we thought that I should first let the detainees get used to my presence. The plan was to attend a church service first.

My first church services with prisoners in Zoetermeer

Because I was playing the pan flute, the pastor asked me if I wanted to take the instrument with me. *Playing the pan flute in prison!* On Sunday morning I am standing in front of the main entrance in a disabled parking space. I thought I could call the doorman via my Bluetooth with voice recognition. Unfortunately, I first had to press number 1 or 2.

My phone, however, only hung in the back of the car near my wheelchair. I struggled with the car for a while. A security guard who was just doing the rounds saw me and helped me further. That's how I came in.

I Waited for by pastor Jean-Pierre and a volunteer Fenna. Three more volunteers arrived later. We took the elevator. From the bottom to the top I passed several doors that were all locked behind me. The view from the silence centre where I sat was in a courtyard with high walls and cameras and of course all this through a window with bars. I saw bars everywhere. After an offered snack I went to my place.

The church visitors finally arrive under the guidance of three guards. Almost all, about 30, most of them younger than me. They are Surinamese, Antilleans, Latin Americans, Africans and one or two Dutch people. They politely shook my hand. At that moment they might be putting their best leg forward. Sturdy boys yes, but some with a small heart.

"Let me play some nice songs later, even though they may have made it themselves, some may not even realize why," I thought.

I got an applause after every piece of music.

They almost treated me like porcelain

After the service they could talk to me personally. One prisoner was speechless and hugged me silently, a good gesture. A strong young Antillean came to me. He saw from his cell how hard it was for me in the parking lot. He said, "If I could break my cell, I would have helped you at that time."

When it was said if I generally did not deserve applause, they clapped and shouted. Magnificent. When they said goodbye to me, the other boy said that I was a strong person and still have some faith in people. On that day there was no difference between the able-bodied and the less able-bodied, between the strong and the weak. We were the children of the one Father who had gathered us in Jesus in the service of Pastor Jean-Pierre. In this silence centre we had sung and prayed so that our faith was accompanied by the care for our loved ones, namely the Vulnerable and the people in need.

In a ward, during a tour, the detainees were just as surprised and responded to a wheelchair. No matter how hard they may be on the outside, they almost treated me like china. I hope I can give a kind of different light to their lives.

I was helped on my departure. In total I had been there for four hours. Just before I wanted to step in, we suddenly heard a roar from above a cell. Maybe the boy who had seen me before? We just waved.

Pastor Jean-Pierre then sent me another card. Now I have ended up in a nasty situation in recent months. In addition to my limitations, "I have suffered a complicated leg fracture that will not heal".

I am becoming more and more isolated and no longer receive positive incentives because I feel trapped again.

Furthermore, I now have to leave a lot to others what I used to do myself. I feel trapped with a mind that wants so much and a body that can do so little. More and more often I thought of the day in prison. Would people feel the same way as I do?

I decided to present my situation to Pastor Jean-Pierre and to write a text for the prison pastoral care www.gevangenispastor.nl.

I visit this site regularly. As I write this, I listen to the songs that were sung in the church service.

God will give me an answer to my questions in time and Jesus is my shepherd. Without realizing that, life would have a different value or perhaps no value. I have received this life and I will make something of it too. Thanks in advance to the site of the prison pastors for the publication of my text.

Loneliness Velserbroek 19-07-2016 6:30 pm.

The visit to the prison made me think. I would like to go there again to be able to exchange ideas with the boys, but due to circumstances of both the prison and myself it has not happened yet. What is solitary confinement? The boys I have seen also have joint activities. They have each other. Or is imprisonment with each other also lonely again? These feelings often keep me busy anyway. Being dependent on my disability means that I am never alone and that there is someone there every day for help. My work in giving lectures and demonstrations is for large or smaller groups of people, where I get all the attention with great respect. Yet there are times when I feel terribly lonely. It is as if I am allowed to taste a bit of the facets of life, while I would like to be completely absorbed in it. Moments that I think I can grasp and hold on to for ever, which then prove to be temporary. Dependency involves a great deal of communication. You are automatically considering whether the other person understands you correctly and that you yourself come across as you would like. In the business area, I have been well trained in that because there is a certain distance. But emotions play a more important role in a friendly area. I don't think a business attitude towards friends is appropriate. It sometimes happens unnoticed that I think I can solve my loneliness in such a situation. Taking a foster child who is with me for a day, weekend or week, going out with a friend, making a blind date. Each time there is a lot of dependency in which I take advantage in the first instance. You come closer together faster. But why does it always feel like saying goodbye after a while? I learned to deal with stand out. With youth theatre in which I also had to participate if necessary and would prefer to play the leading role. At concerts with my pan flute as a child. In choirs. The first choir member that stands out is me. But I am used to that attention. I'm not avoiding it either. That would mean that I am ashamed and I will not. How that goes in a relationship 1 on 1 is much more complicated. Because of that dependent position and perhaps because of my open character I have experienced terrible pitfalls. It does not mean that the need is therefore less. Only trust in this is very vulnerable. I will keep looking for 1 on 1 attention, but I think in a way that is safer. By seeing my own desire through someone's eyes leading a very different life. Through the eyes of a trucker, through the eyes and lens of a professional photographer, through the eyes of an African, through the eyes of my closest friend. All reflect my desire and the reflection sometimes makes me dizzy. There is an answer, but only temporarily. I taste it and desire. Then I would like to hold it forever. Attention 1 to 1. But how much confidence is needed for that. This realization makes me lonely. Not being alone. At such moments I need my creativity all the more and that is the only way to understand my feelings.

Unexpectedly I was able to attend a drawing course in the east of the country last week. I was among the people again and received attention that I am used to. The hours of concentrated drawing made my mind calm again. The forest walks and nature gave me the calmness of a creation, of more. Maybe I'm never alone.

Let me be an artist! Velserbroek 07-09-2016 23: 41h.

How they always find me again is a surprise every time. But I can respond just as surprisingly as that. I was told by telephone from the Princess Beatrix Fund that they had been in existence for 60 years and that it would be an honour for me to be present. Not just present, but to exhibit and demonstrate in a beautifully created place with paintings and other materials. It was to take place in the Beatrix Theatre, followed by a TV show that I was invited to attend. Her Majesty would also pay a visit. Well with 2 days for reflection I had no problem with that. I have the car loaded the next day. Easels were taken care of. Nice to set up the paintings. I took a suitcase with illustrations of which I had quickly made some extras, a drawing table and my books supplemented. Who knows, I could offer Bea one more. So, when I arrived to unload, the theatre was already surrounded by security. Inside, there were mainly exhibitors in the scientific field who are subsidized by the Princess Beatrix Fund. My share was, I believe, a welcome change and a bit of entertainment for everyone present. In the morning part, something happened in the theatre. That way I could make a draft of my paintwork. When the break came and the doors opened right in front of me to give people the opportunity to have lunch, their attention was drawn to my painter.

In no time it was full of enthusiastic people around who looked at everything, admired it, talked to me and also bought works from me. I have been able to sign practically every booklet that I have sold. This continued almost uninterruptedly until the afternoon part. Unbelievable. And then there was the spectacular show and a drink or other drink afterwards. But when I was back in the car, that car that drives me everywhere I go whenever I want, no matter how old it gets, I thought it was a pity that I could not speak to Her Majesty, because even though she is ours she had little to say about her trip. She is also being lived. And that is my great fear that, that will happen to me when my car abandons me and has to be rejected. I have to give up more and more in terms of independence due to my muscular disease. And if this muscle disease had been the culprit that I would no longer be able to drive, I would have had to resign myself to it. But so far, my clinical picture has no influence on my driving behaviour. At the moment there is simply nobody that could possibly pay for the adjustments. Less than two weeks later I came up with this problem on TV myself. A home-made video showing as many cheerful images as possible and where I explain my concern in 1 minute. 'Man, bites dog' wanted to support me in this by sending it out. Even though I had known my own video for a long time, it made me very aware how close this problem is. Is a rescue attempt after this? I want so much to remain the artist who meets so many people, who does not have to say 'no', who stands out because of the drive for independence and is at the centre of life. If only they understood that in politics.

Let me be an artist, let me be human.

Chapter 4

Arrangement Texel ends in drama Velserbroek 26-10-2016 14: 35h.

For business it seemed nice to me to go to Texel and immediately combine several things. For example, I wanted to visit a former rehabilitation person who I got to know in 1995 and who I helped with a service dog. He wrote a book about his dog, or actually on behalf of his dog, which I personally wanted to pick up. I also wanted to visit some family who live there and finally after several promises I wanted to exhibit my work in one of the hotels in Den Burg. By the way, I was staying at another hotel where I was not going to exhibit. But even before I was on Texel, everything went wrong. Just that weekend before a collision. I was not even there myself, because I was having a nice party at the Haven festival where I also had a performance with my choir. There were friends from all over the country. The weather was beautiful. Once back at the parking lot, I found my car there with a very dented tailgate and killed window. Then I was advised to call in the police to make a report. Indeed, an anonymous tip of the registration number of the opposing party had already been passed on to the police. Well, the next day. One day before departure. Telephone maintenance with insurance. Had information to which claims company I had to go. It was difficult for me to keep driving with such a hole in the back, then I gassed. So immediately here 12 km away, but the tailgate and the window were too damaged. Parts had to be ordered for that. Then forwarded to Carglass again 7 km back for an emergency solution. So, no more gases in the car. Quickly home for the hairdresser. That evening I got a flat tire from my wheelchair. That too. I could wait until the next morning. I called again the next morning and instead of the rehabilitation technicians there came lazy from a bicycle mechanic. I like it, as long as they did their job, so that we could go to Texel preferably this day. Finally, after feeding ourselves (Pierre and I), having given the dogs a drink and having a bunch of starlings begging to enjoy while waiting for the boat, the crossing could begin. The cosy family hotel was easy to find. The room was a bit on the tight side and the door size was, in my opinion, from the 18th century, because the wheelchair did not fit. A few steps then. Good for my condition. Having my anti-decubitus air mattress borrowed on a trial, because of my back pain, to be able to be rocked as a little princess in the nights by the moving air cells. Seated on the sunny terrace for dinner and a moderate Texel breeze taken an Aperitivo to recover from the hectic pace before. In the evening hung on a bar decorated in a living room and was introduced to fellow hotel guests. The entertainment newspaper caught to see what else there was to do in the coming days in addition to my regular appointments. There was a crafts market. The next day I went to the former rehabilitant to get the book about the assistance dog and I also gave my book. Further on the list was also buying a sheep wool saddle covers for mom, dad and sister. I treated myself to a little sheep that you can use by trough a Velcro cushion. Nice for under my arm in bed. The first day passed. My second cousin, living on Texel, also came to the hotel for dinner one evening with his girlfriend. Then I dived into a cafe that was familiar to him, where I drank my favourite drink 'Texels Juttertje'. My second cousin did my PR immediately he did business to be able to exhibit my paintings there with the request to also have a look at my site. Also, to see my work, but he is the webmaster. Nice, another goal. That made it pretty late. Oops! If only the hotel were open now! But the guests, old people and young people were fortunately all-night owls. The next day we first took a brisk walk with the dogs, so that they could relax in the bedroom and we could freshen up a bit in the bathroom. The last evening, I wanted to go to my second cousin. The tiles in the bathroom seemed super non-slip so they felt stiff, in a dry state. I thought it would be wise to walk sideways with my back along the wall, as I felt wetness, back to my wheelchair. I only went sideways when the trouble started. Suddenly there was a tense atmosphere. The floor was suddenly slippery that I slid into splits in no time. Ahh! I got a huge pain in my left thigh. Immediately I could tell from the stand that it had to be broken. Like a soccer player, I lay moaning on the floor with my head almost at the hinge of the door that had to open inwards to me. Oh? damn, there we go again. How do I get out of here now? Panic! The reception informed 112 quickly to call. Whether I had become unwell? Not yet, but if they don't get along.

Sing, fight, cry, pray Velserbroek 17-12-2016 19: 58h.

In order to cancel after so many agreements, I wanted to stimulate the feeling of progress in myself and to overcome the doubts to participate in a hobby market and to give a reading one afternoon. A friend of mine with a modified bus drove me. Pierre stayed specially with me all weekend. The days before I was a bit tense. Could I sit for so long? Shall I paint? The night was messy. The day started very early. I was not allowed to take a step and with two people I had to be helped out of bed with a hoist. So, before I'm well and truly in my wheelchair... The hobby market was close by and so quite a few acquaintances came by that I had not seen for a short or sometimes long time with the usual question how I was doing. It always made me aware how I was not. I decided to put a lot on paper and with that to withdraw into my own world.

A few more weeks, I thought, then maybe I can do everything again. The paintings became beautiful, suggestive, bold. My character. I could have them framed as a series, created during injury time. A difficult time in which something beautiful can still be created. My story on the lecture also gave me encouraging words. That we did it for a while despite the situation. But I also don't feel sick and that's why I want so much.

The check in the hospital was coming. A trainee could take part from the assistance. I had a little claim. I felt good and expected a good answer. That answer was only disappointing. There was hardly any bone formation in my leg. What now? Continue with home therapy, rehabilitation? How long will this joke last after nine weeks? The advice was to be careful to stimulate the leg by burdening it with crutches of course. How scary it was and how tough it was in the beginning. But I would walk! I wanted to make progress now. My car is just a bit beautiful at the door. With a van I try to find entertainment elsewhere. It takes time. Such a ride is collective, so from A, B, C to D. It costs energy because of thresholds, potholes in those detours, which causes me back and neck problems again. But I want to get out. Get on stage. Although I had missed a lot of the choir rehearsals, I was on schedule for our anniversary show in the theatre. I had nine guests for that evening. That evening I wanted to honour the name of our choir. Sparkle, I wanted to shine that night. At that place I could forget everything again. Singing and absorbing what I sang. Enjoy the reactions of the enthusiastic audience. Hard work, but satisfying. I cannot let myself be restrained. I can't ride. I am a thoroughbred with temperament for that. I want to get started, because the process is a race and I want to win.

From oppressive stuffiness to limitless freedom at home 23-06-2017 22: 15h.
"It will be your first and also your last car" was said 20 years ago, after I received my first car, an Opel Kadett caravan with hydraulic joystick steering, via the municipality with a lot of fuss. The car that I always gave a pat on the back, because it brought me safely to my destinations.

As an artist I started to master mouth painting with my parents. Here and there everywhere and nowhere I was taken to my exhibitions. Time and again you could find me somewhere on the road. But once I became known I had to go into the wide world. My artist life expanded enormously after my move to my own home. I became more daring and got guts. Let me go. I'll get there.

Two to three times a month I gave presentations about my work somewhere in the country with sometimes even an overnight stay arranged for me. My assistance dog also went everywhere with me. When I was home to take it easy and to paint, I was always found for a new appointment. There were radio interviews where I could come to the studio. Whether I also wanted to participate in a TV broadcast with Henk Schiffmacher. Of course, I still have a car to drive to the NPO in Hilversum. And so, I suddenly found myself in the midst of artists such as Suzan and Monique Cleman, Ronnie Tober, Barry Hey, Louise van Tuylingen, Sandra Brood and a number of others. And that is how I ended up as a VIP in the nightclub Panama, where famous artists such as Herman Brood were auctioned and where there actually was and was auctioned between my paintings.

The pleasure I got from this led me to look for photographers to do photo shoots with me and I did an online audition and then started working as a model. What prevented me from making a blind date with someone. Meet somewhere halfway along the route. Crazy! All with my own transport.

The Opel was now twelve years old but in good condition for the time being. What about this car, what should I do without? An application was submitted to the municipality to get the ball rolling. But the municipality issued a negative opinion. I felt myself sinking into the deep. Everything I developed and reached could I just not drop it?

I received more hits from this blow. An operation on my back was necessary and sometime later it was a hip placement. Boarding became considerably difficult. I couldn't get my wheelchair in independently anymore. Fortunately, I could be helped with that. The Opel was now almost seventeen years old. Over time my balance became less and less. I decided to appeal. There will really have to be a new car. With a broken arm of another fall I was in the courtroom. Apparently, it made no impression on the judge. I lost the appeal. It didn't get any better. A few years later I fell seriously and suffered a complicated leg fracture again. My willpower was put to the test. The Opel was parked in the parking lot of the rehabilitation centre. I could only look at it, but couldn't get into it. Although I should crawl into it. I had to think of something for myself. I designed a brace for the weak leg. And with a red satin pillowcase against the rubber edge of the door I slid into the car with a lot of moans. My father sometimes pulled the demolition over my head. Occasionally a joke. "Little Red Riding Hood where are you going?" I kept it that way for a while.

At a presentation I was told that I had something to come for. 'Some?' I thought. "You should know!"

Others thought it was crazy to say that I didn't get a new car. It took me a lot of energy. A final attempt was to send in a video with my story. Four responses were received. The courage sank in my shoes, but my agenda was still completely full. I had to ask for more help on the spot. I became depressed with fatigue. Many friends sympathized and were just as powerless. Until a girlfriend, who is known at B&S special garage, told my story there. We just had to sit around the table together and see what would be possible for me. It sounded very interesting.

'Space-drive joystick', Mercedes Sprinter. Yes, Yes. Do I have to drive a bus like this? Everything was still dizzy. Now, however, I could remain in my wheelchair if it were to continue with that bus. Every time I had visited B&S again and made custom adjustments, I saw a bright spot again and I got air. I dared to look into the future again. Wouldn't it be handy to get sponsors? This had to succeed. With the help of my friends, we succeeded in recruiting sponsors. Still succeed in recruiting sponsors. The conversion of the Mercedes Sprinter grew. I was surprised that I was going to be the driver. Twelve extra habituation lessons were included. And then, 'on the worst day of the year with shop power nine and a box of rain' I had to take my driving test for the CBR if necessary. But with a bottle of wine gift I drove home. From that time there was music again. A lot is being driven again. My life is back on track. A music is on with guitar music. The suitcases with things are on the chair, my dog is in the back seat.

When I open the window to say hello to my assistant, she asks, "Paris?" I drive away laughing.

The wind drove me to the North Velserbroek 10-10-2016 10:44 pm.
It has often happened that I discussed or tried to put into words the amazing experience of half a year ago with my Frisian trucker buddy. The unconditional trust in each other as strangers then, dependence. Fear on my part to be 'present' too much and on the other hand perhaps to fail in care. In the time that followed, I had also kept quiet. Of course, I had become curious about how he is leading his life and how he is in life. The thought of the connection with us and the unexpected invitation, after a comment from me as a joke or missing me that was somewhat confirmed to come to the Frisian country, encouraged me. An additional question was whether I could provide home care for a few days. We had discovered that taking care of everything physically and mentally was not possible either. Well, everyone has his profession. I found all the questions together serious enough to answer. I had never arranged it that way before, and at first, I didn't know which way to go. Four agencies were involved. A Central indication agency, a care office from this region, a care office from Friesland and finally

the Frisian home care where I actually had to request six weeks in advance, but for once it was possible in five weeks. Five weeks to prepare spiritually. I found the whole situation exciting. The fact that this kid is always on his own and alone is taking me home with my whole being and hold. You literally cannot get around me. Bed in the living room, dog that can sometimes get in the way so well and 'the lady of the house' for which the furniture had to be moved to make room for the wheelchair. Then the person must be very busy with me in mind. The neighbours were also informed. The neighbour at the back door had made a wooden entrance and exit at the back door and I myself had a cord with a rubber ball on the door handle so that Luigi could open the door. First of all, to save myself as much as possible and I knew that I would be moments alone. He went to bed for night shifts or for groceries. But I thought it was just that I was allowed to spend a couple of nights with someone who has such a different life and those few days that had to put a little bit aside, had to adapt to the help I needed. Enjoying that company together. Not alone for a moment. Talk, ask questions. It is quite different. The home care was good professional and punctual. I often got the same person and they all enjoyed the situation. Also, how we got to know each other. If I had my Frisian sugar bun ready in the morning and I went walking with the dog very well, I would just have a good feeling. Everything went so well. I was fairly independent anyway and I felt less burdened asking for 'small' help. And what could be better than if you were ready to go to bed, someone would come and sit on the edge and want to do something nice and cosy. I was grateful for it, I also told him; "Nobody takes it away from me." In those few days, the nicest attention there was. To be continued???

How to make children happy Velserbroek 11-30-2016 3:03 pm.
I regularly give a lecture at schools and my enthusiastic stories about it led to one of the employees of our housing project inviting her daughter to make her birthday party very special. It had been planned for months and all her girlfriends, who did not yet know the details, were burning with curiosity about what awaited them. With my own entrance gutters, the artist entered herself with some fiddling and all eyes were on me. But not for long, because Luigi also drew the necessary attention and after asking whether they were all looking forward to it, the joy of their desserts radiated. All preparations had already been made. They were ready to go. First, I had to get something on paper myself. For the children I had some examples with me, but apparently, they didn't need that. Their imagination was big enough and they all preferred to come up with something themselves. Real artists. What the hell was I supposed to do? I knew what would appeal to those girls at that age - horses. That's a while since I signed it! I was also possessed by horses at that age. I have horse-riding for 20 years and when it

started to hurt too much, I sat behind it and followed a short driving course to be able to ride a horse and cart. A pity that I had to undergo operations, because it was really a great sport, because there are also competitions in it. Anyway, I had to get that horse in my imagination now. What were those beautiful illustrations of a book 'The roaring horse' from Rien Poortvliet. I just started somewhere. Soon there were such astonished reactions that I felt it would be okay. While I was busy with my horse, all the tassels went in the mouth. They were all working diligently. In between, my progressing horse was watched with great enthusiasm and that was a great incentive to continue with all of us. Some could barely stop even though the hot sausage rolls were already on the table. When the sandwiches were finished and all the artworks had dried a little, they all wanted to take a picture with me proudly. The children happy and so do I, because there is nothing better than to give joy to a child.

Velserbroek city bus Chipcard 22-01-2017 21: 45h.

A few times I noticed that there was a wheelchair sticker on the Connexxion city buses, but when I saw passengers getting in and out, I wondered how a wheelchair should be put in. The only way to find out was to ask the driver. According to him, a board unfolded and I, even without a companion, could take the bus. Immediately I thought of swimming. I hate wheelchair transportation. You can never count on it. From the city bus though. Previously, therefore, I had been using the wheelchair for about three years, 5 km there and back, due to wind and weather. For safety's sake, I wanted to do this experiment on the way back, should it go wrong. There I was at the bus stop. For the first time in my life I have a chipcard in my hands waiting for it to be used. Three buses passed me. I'm not having fun in such a booth, am I? Someone came to me. I kindly asked if he would inform the driver that I also wanted to go. "I could have been home already," I thought. There he was. Line 73. I looked out my eyes. With a lot of rattling a driver came back. That rumble was the money box, otherwise it is stolen from it. He reached out to the floor with one hand and grabbed a hand grip and actually a board flipped out with which I drove into the bus, also to the admiration of the occupants. "Just stand up as usual," said the driver. Automatically, I naturally just stood with my head in the direction of travel. That was wrong. So, I had to stand backwards in a reserved wheelchair place with my back against the back of the normal chair. A belt on my left under the window was just stretched over my backrest to limit curves and to the right of me an extra armrest was folded down to prevent tipping. My bus journey could start and I enthusiastically laughed at the fellow passengers. The bus was nice and warm and the ride took less than 10 minutes. Still, I was concerned about how I can get the driver's attention in the dark that I want to come with, because I cannot raise my arm. My father still had a plastic orange flag from a bike ride with all the beer names on it. Well what a calling card I care. From the kitchen I saw him dangling in the shed to put in a suitable plastic stick. The job was done and with an imitation of a seriously physically deficient he came out with the flag in his hand. Would they take me at all? I was already laughing at seeing my father, let alone sitting there with the flag in my wheelchair. I'll use it anyway in extreme need. But it remains an adventure. I had a good grasp of the routine of running in and screwing in. Neatly I had said again where I wanted to go. Assuming that the driver would keep an eye on that, I suddenly saw my bus stop by. "Hey, I got to get out!" I cried. "Hey, she has to get out!" Others shouted like a kind of echo. "Shit!" I hear in the front. Yes, where do you park the bus on the main road to the centre? Only parked cars by the side. Then at the first the best side street. The bus stopped in the middle of the road. A guilty passenger who was in a deep conversation with the driver helped with all his might. No sidewalk or nothing. A very steep exit. I already saw a long line of cars' with probably curious people thinking what is going on now. An invalid with a leather hat and long raincoat? But actually, quite comical, definitely not boring.

Afternoon nap but no trick Velserbroek 24-04-2017 9:20 pm.

Something has been nibbling in me for months. It started with some nasty back pain. I blamed the many and distant driving. But on quiet days it did not go away. Complaints were added. In the evening I woke up with the pain of breathing. I was not really comfortable with this. First, I had X-rays made of my spine with the thought that it hopefully had to do with a fusion. But at first glance the orthopaedist could see few strange changes. Giving my body only three months left according to him. But because of the sleepless nights, I wanted a stronger painkiller. A few days I slept a hole in the day, until the complaints came back. Not only with sleeping, but now also with singing and speaking, which I love doing so much. Then back in the medical mill. Blood test. My veins already jump away at the idea. I ended up on the recovery without being operated. A very nice nurse immediately provided a complete bed. Gosh, and that to drain blood. But that was because of the difficult to find veins. I wondered if I had them. The anaesthesiologist felt nothing but a vein. The carotid artery still. Quite a tour. The same tour had to be done again for a few days, due to a drip that had to be laid. However, the cooperation was missing this time. Such a long scan with contrast fluid was only done upon admission. The stress had made me so cold that the same friendly nurse pampered me again. He got heated blankets and stopped me. Even though I could leave after half an hour. So, let me take up again a few days later. Three times is right. But not much wiser. Put a lot of money into it myself. Tempur pillow, mattress and cushion purchased for the wheelchair. I could not get to sleep. How should I proceed? Apart from the afternoon nap, I really couldn't sit still. The more miserable I started to feel, the more I wanted to leave. Anyway, I had appointments in abundance for the lectures. I had a nice proposal, also for my parents, to go from now in the afternoon to lectures to avoid the traffic jams and make it a fun day. I did drive. Awesome. And then my parents' comments on the English-speaking navigator that I just called James. Dad who really has no knowledge of it and says so confidently that James will drop you at the door. And just like my mother wants to say something and we hear 'recalculation' for the umpteenth time, 'gps signal lost' she grumbles: 'can't that guy keep his mouth shut? he just wants to have something to say!' Then I am enjoying myself at the wheel. Fortunately, I forgot my pain and especially the worries about it. One evening after a long drive, someone knocked on the car window when I parked. It turned out to be the host family of my previous dog Nero. Twenty seven years ago. I only recognized her when she said her name. She had the portrait photo of mine and Nero back then. She could not deny that it was me, because to my surprise I saw in the photo that I was wearing the same blouse again that night. As if I had nothing new. But it was so comfortable. At another daytime lecture, where I did go alone, I was welcomed by homeless people. Oh well, they are only people and this was very special for them. To help me out of the car.

I told all this during an interview at home by a reporter for BNN. He became so enthusiastic about my stories and my enthusiasm that while reporting with the brush in his mouth he tried to get something on paper and tell about it at the same time. How nice it is to find such a balance with all those experiences, art and encounters in relation to the pain that might be answered.

Never hide your talents   Velserbroek 01-07-2017 3:46 pm.

It started sixty years ago. A disabled young man with paralyzed arms did not want to be an attraction, but a real artist. He followed various artistic courses and qualified as a painter who painted by mouth. His fame prompted other disabled artists to gain the same motivation and inspiration, and more and more artists were added worldwide. I myself have been around for 30 years. Because of this 60-year anniversary, I was also invited to travel with one companion for a week to the beautiful city of Barcelona where the entire hotel was rented for 400 guests from this club. I had a special wish to have a friend [known as 'magic man'] experience this event because of both his and my and our turbulent life in the past year in which I myself have discovered a nice growth with regard to care as the peace and quiet and relaxation associated with this. A wonderful travel companion and he just had to experience this. Really nice contact. Not with disabled people, but simply with full-fledged people who will also have fought to become artists and want to be recognized as such. We all dealt with each other as such in whatever language. The program was really taken care of. As many as 12 coaches left under escort to various places of interest. That only meant that we got up every morning at 6 o'clock to catch bus 1, which left at 8.30 am without mercy. But it was very worthwhile. In the morning there was always a reception with a coffee table and in the afternoon via catering with delicious snacks and drinks. We were really spoiled. The program also included a beautiful boat trip and the Gala Dinner. Really amazing. But all week long I realized that almost anybody with disabilities had to deal with almost anything and that I am very happy to be part of that. It is very stimulating that you are almost 1 large family. You all have a goal; become and remain an artist. And through this association, some people have been able to develop multiple talents. Books have been written. Painting therapy is given. Very impressive. That is why I want to tackle everything that has to do with an artistic world, because it is also such a special means of communication. Not only can you say something non-verbally with paintings, but also with music and with my new discovery; model photography. I had an online audition for fun and I just came back from Barcelona and read the email that I could visit a photo studio in Zwolle. A unique opportunity that they also granted me that I am just human [and what kind of]. Can I still be seen? I cannot always say what I am and feel on the inside as a model. This will not be the last time either. You should not bury talents but use them [bible: Math 18:22].

The new resident Velserbroek 17-02-2018 20: 11h.

Half a year ago I started participating in a hobby market with the prospect that things would soon be better. I had even risked crutches a bit. However, no progress was seen on the X-rays, even until recently. In November I was already a bit burdensome in the hope that bone production could be accelerated. I also visited a rehabilitation hospital nearby. There, however, no help could be offered to such a patient as me, but the rehabilitation doctor there certainly promised me that he would get me into the rehabilitation centre. Nothing happened. My thoughts formed an increasingly hopeless situation. Also, because in the meantime someone was working on it and there was no clarity. For weeks I am already very dependent. I can hardly use my arms while sitting. Days are starting to look more and more the same. TV, PC and some painting. Too cold and too bad weather to go out for a detour. Grief prevails that my lively, enthusiastic and adventurous spirit was now trapped in this body that has paralyzed me in less than a second. Not for a while, but for, I know a lot, how long. Everywhere I used to be, I now seem almost forgotten. In December I had an abscess in my stomach with which I had to go up and down to the hospital for 5 days initially with a wheelchair van that first went off town and country and the driver asked halfway through the ride: "Which side of Rotterdam should you be precise? " I was shocked (Rotterdam south of Holland I live in the north). "Rotterdam? I have to go to Velserbroek!" So, Mom and I decided next time to take the city bus again, which also stopped at the hospital. Did I still want to spend a midweek break with my girlfriend in a care hotel? Fortunately, I did that. We were served by professional help, the food was great, we participated in workshops and together we gave a demonstration with our dogs one evening for a group of mentally handicapped people.

Because I still can't drive myself, I have to let myself be driven. Drivers already make the remark whether I have just come to live here, because they had never driven me. In fact, I now feel like a different person. More and more I am withdrawing myself, because if I want to explain to friends how I really feel, I get well-meant reactions, reactions that I should not let my head down, publishers never win and winners never give up, old Hanneke wants to be. This way I no longer have the space to be myself, the Hanneke who wants to make something clear, that it is not going well, that I am going to get lost in powerlessness and insecurity, that I feel so trapped. To get a hold of things, I even contacted the justice ministry to explain my feelings, also because a few years ago I myself attended a prison service with prisoners to play the pan flute. This story was considered impressive and I was instructed to write an article about it for the bay site www.gevangenispastor.nl, in which I explain how I came in contact at the time, how I felt then with prisoners and especially what I felt at this time. moment feels. To be honest, that kind of relieved. I also informed my doctor about my fears and sorrows. I need someone who understands me and who not only listens to my grief, but also dares to behold it. Many people cannot or do not dare to confront. The new occupant no longer knows what to do with the situation and wants to stand with both feet on the ground again, but she cannot do it alone. In two days, I can finally go to the rehabilitation centre again Heliomare. I hope to be able to go upstream there. Let's go!

Bus driving lessons Hoorn 19-03-2018 13: 12h.
On my way to Hoorn to see my bus. And yes, there it was, the white Mercedes Sprinter with the big sticker SOLD on the front. Inside it was still bald. The carcass is actually covered with wood. No seats, nothing. I thought the passenger seat. Then the driver ... "Me." It was soon discovered that I came up with my knees against the steering wheel because of the rising floor at the front. Unfortunately. Then just a bus, intended for another, driven in with a lowered bottom. So, it should be, a lot of work.

19-06-2018 13: 00h.
Boy, how those people have been hard at work. You could still see the wiring. The sport steering wheel was also already there. Awkward in such a jack of a bus. In my Opel there is

also one and so one garage owner once asked the window in wonder: "So, you raced too?" Of course, … with a station car. "No, this is the steering wheel, the joystick." Even bigger eyes.

The height and the way of accommodation to me was investigated. The correct angle of the belt. The height of the headrest that will turn towards me electrically from the side. What a technique! Soon I will be on the road again…

The bus is almost ready. The lessons are mainly intended to experience how it works in such a bus and to adjust the adjustments optimally, which I am honestly working on today [grr]. At the 1st lesson, only the brake and steering controls were different than with my Opel. That was noticeable too! What a sensitive system. It was much too light for me. The bus looked like a tumbler. So, it went on for a while. There is also a small computer in it. They, the engineers, can only log in to adjust the electronics. I only read the warnings or commands and execute them. I think I have had about 8 lessons. before I could take the bus home. I had to take a test drive for the CBR. And yes, that test was on the day with the worst weather conditions to take a bus from Hoorn to Velserbroek for the first time. Storm, strong gusts of wind, rain. I had to drive for half an hour and … I succeeded. While I waited in the bus, they tried to persuade me to drive home another day, but my decision was certain. Suddenly a bottle of red wine came as a gift. I felt really happy. My own bus, my unlimited mobility. I want to look beyond the horizon again.

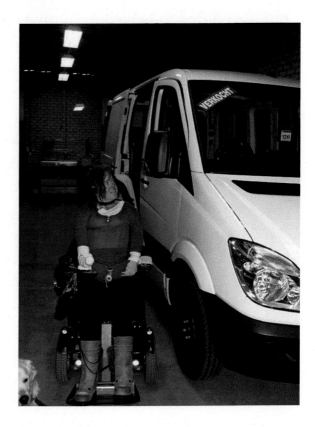

Autumn

Autumn
changes my colours
like no rainbow has got.

It is autumn
which makes my leaves
able to fly.

Seasons I have waited
for this flight.
The moment of a free fall.

And I know
it is autumn.
I am going to die.

Son of God

I'm on my way to a stable.
Houses seem to me too fine.
I've heard a child is born
under the stars they shine.

Searching this child, the King,
thy angels, thy shepherds, where's everything?
Jesus, shall I feel thy love?
You Son of God above.

Is it the truth they tell?
How do you get so well?
Walk with them the long way.
Maybe one moment I will say:

I'm on my way to a stable.
Houses seem to me too fine.
I know a King is born
under the stars they shine.

Raindrop

Sometimes I hear a very sweet sound.
It's falling regular with echoes to the ground.

I'm curious about it but never looked and see.
I keep waiting, thinking who's teasing me.

But last week I did have a look behind.
It was a simple raindrop dancing so kind.

It attracted my attention away,
because it was worried if it would come back some day.

And I couldn't catch it before,
because than it wouldn't dance anymore.

Guide

I discovered a voice.
A voice in me.
A good friend
and the best guide
there ever will be.

No stranger.
Not just someone.
No voyager,
but when it says
it is:

It is not a joke.
It is a journey
when you listen
to your guide.
Your promise.

Tears

I can feel them now
in my eyes burning.
They now let me feel
that they are yearning

to twinkle beside

my nose
so that I can taste them,
hear them falling close.

Tears, tears, tears
I have waited too long.
After your weakness
I can feel so strong.

I shall enjoy you
at a silent place.
Just the two of us.
Face to face.

We can make it.
Together
like a sun in
Rainy weather.

Desire

Don't leave me please.
Our time is short
in this precious moment.
Don't release.

Because I feel worthen
when you're here with me.
There's so much value in my life,
cause of your love I can see.

I'm impressed of your kindness.
You set my heart on fire.
The emotion so truly and nice.
I cannot live without my desire.

Please don't go
'till our hearts meet each other
and will share the passion.
Oh, how I do love you so.

Garden song

The seed I'd throwing
are flowers now growing.
The lark sings on high.

Between their smell,
between its beauty,
here stand I.

Enjoying this nature
with her plants and creatures.
They can be so small.

While watching I
seem like a giant.

67

For these creatures so tall.

I'm not afraid
and count on their faith.
There is no fear.

Try to remember
we're all natures member.
I'm so happy to be here.

On fire

I look dreamy
out through the window.
The evening is coming.

A candle fire,
romance sounds in music.
In a flash it is thoughts that go.

The child in me ran
to participate in the game.
The younger was looking for adventure.

Muscle strength seems to be weakening.
The bones become brittle.
My flame is almost frightened by intense fire.

Because now I want to be on fire.
My heart is running wild for you.
There is no time waiting.

To be able to love you
and to melt for your heat.

Take me if it's for one night!

I want to win from the pain.
Forget my worries,
if I lie by your side.

The energy you have
gives me strength.
My flame is burning, ignite me!

My beauty is harder to find
in a body that wants less and less.
A touch of loving power.

Now that I am capable of it
to give me completely.
Set me on fire even if it's for one night!

Love

A nice gesture,
a sweet smile.
The sun in the house,
a fun day.

No hand that shakes,
an arm around me.
Not just a shoulder,
but salvaged, one together.

A desire so intense,
which can sadden me for a moment.
So beautiful, so short.

I can only taste it.

Always looking
to Him who gives me love.
If I may carry it out forever,
is it the love that lives in me?

So many tears are full of love,
too many tears are full of sorrow.
Oh God, how do I love You?
with all my soul, feeling and heart!

Only you

That is how love should be
without doubts and unrestrained,
without prejudice or pain.

Although there seem to be such differences
in every living creature, but
no being would want without love.

I would like to give you this love.
Sincere love with all my soul,
all my heart, all my life.

Like dolphins in the sea
and seagulls on the beach.
Never alone, but with two.

When the soft down chick
basks with a goat
I caress you, rejoice.

The cups of lion and lioness.
A giraffe kisses the squirrel.

I believe in this love.

I also believe in you.
More and more, deeper and deeper
even though the world now seems grey.

Are you giving me a chance?
In this difficult world.
Can I have this dance?

As a dog I am so loyal.
I will sleep with you and watch over you.
My love, my love I love you.

Eric's boat

A shining moon
a twinkling star
the dark clear sky.

Love is growing,
bodies we're showing
my heart beats and thy

velvet fingers.
A hand that lingers.
holding my head.

Screaming to me.
Begging to me:
'make love until death'.

We can hear no sea.
We can see no waves.
Everything disappears.

His lips meeting my lips,

tasting the flesh.
Warmed, happiness, no fears.

We are the sea.
Move like the waves.
Naked under his coat.

Two people together,
being one.
Happened on Eric's boat.

Best friend

Thinking about you is so incredibly beautiful.
Our friendship is always, however.
I never felt any closer
by your heat that I defrost.
Not just my cold arms,
but the secrets of my soul
opens because of your attention, that I fell
for the wonderful moments that really heat up.
I wouldn't miss a day with you.
Skipping days become dreams
about those times that I want to come to you.
Only I cannot decide that.
Never has anyone cared so much for me.
I needed you so badly, even in difficult times
when you were so sad and in pain
on very critical days, the most difficult of your life.
Then at such a moment you would be standing
in front of my door
touches me so deep inside.
You care so much about me, I am your best friend.

If you ever fall, I'll never let you go
and I'll never leave you alone again.
Until that time, I keep expressing myself.
Beautiful words from love to delight you.
Because as you are, there is none

Winter

The winter feels very chilly.
Thoughts slip away
to some warmth and love,
because it is quiet around me.

The winter gives cold.
I seem to be withdrawing
not to wander in the dark,
but actually, I long for you.

Winter has memories,
in which you surprised me.
You are blinding like the snow,
That's why I love to hold you.

The winter gets a different face
of a lit candle in the night
that makes my eyes shine bright
and then suddenly relieves all cold and silence.

The winter gets a glow
across the cold, snowy land.
Where icy drops are like pearls
they twinkle when your heart meets mine.

The winter also passes.
A whole year is closed.
Except for all the moments of us together.
They remain as a jewel for you and me ...

Never be lost

When the sun no longer wants to glow
and the flowers don't bloom.
My love for you will never be lost!

If my powers are taken away,
fear and doubt come back for it.
My love for you will never be lost!

When my pains will sting
and colours thereby fade.
My love for you will never be lost!

If I ever lose my way.
Then don't sleep, keep watching over me.
My love for you will never be lost!

If I should ever die
then I will be reborn again.
My love for you will never be lost!

Printed in the United States
by Baker & Taylor Publisher Services